Start Investing in Crypto

Start Investing in Crypto

A beginner's no-hype guide to safely buying and holding digital assets.

Rowan Hale

Mindful Pages

Published in 2025

ISBN: 9789371772679 (PB)
ISBN: 9789371772549 (eBook)

Published by

Mindful Pages
Imprint of Alpha Editions LLC
312 W. 2nd St #1834
Casper, WY 82601, USA

This book was developed using advanced writing tools to support the drafting and ideation process. All content has been thoughtfully curated, refined, and reviewed to ensure quality and relevance.

Content

Introduction
Reclaiming Sanity in a Digital Gold Rush

Something about this present moment feels uncanny. On one hand, we are in the midst of a financial shift so vast that future chroniclers may well call it a second Renaissance of value. On the other, we are caught in a storm of noise—half-truths, showmanship, algorithmic chatter—that makes the act of clear judgment feel like a lost art. For many, crypto appears either as a ticket to sudden fortune or as a murky box filled with jargon, frauds, and speculation run wild. What it is seldom introduced as, though, is what it may truly represent: a quiet revolution in trust, ownership, and personal sovereignty.

This book is not a manual for wealth-chasing. That field is already saturated. Scroll through shelves, digital or physical, and you will see promises of easy riches, graphs climbing without restraint, influencers selling salvation in a few bullet points. What is conspicuously absent is a space for reflection—for patience, perspective, and depth.

You are holding something different. A guide that recognises the volatility of markets is only a surface expression of a deeper volatility within ourselves: our impulses, our habits, our restless need for meaning. Crypto is not merely an asset class. It is a mirror. And whether that mirror reflects opportunity or anxiety, clarity or confusion, depends less on what tokens you purchase than on the kind of investor—and person—you are becoming.

This book, then, is about cultivating digital self-trust in an era increasingly mediated by abstraction. It is about building the discipline not to react, the philosophical sharpness to grasp what you truly own, and the moral strength to hold both assets and attention with intention. If that sounds almost monastic, so be it. The central thesis here is stark: stillness, not speed, is your competitive advantage.

We are not here to sell coins. We are here to offer a compass.

The clamour around crypto is not accidental—it is engineered. Platforms, influencers, and protocols alike are invested in keeping your attention twitching, your decisions reactive. The design is not new; it is the same logic that keeps slot machines spinning, social feeds infinite, and financial news relentless. In volatility, urgency becomes the performance. Everyone is shouting. But perhaps you need not raise your voice at all.

This book asks you to do something rarer: lower the volume. To develop the most undervalued quality in the crypto world—equanimity.

Equanimity is not surrender. It is composure. It is the steadiness to assess risk without letting fear take the wheel, the grace to meet innovation without discarding caution, the strength to act—rather than flinch—amid uncertainty. Markets may writhe; your mind need not.

Why crypto, and why now? Because something fundamental is underway, whether or not you join it. We are watching trust itself decentralise. For centuries, value has been anchored by institutions—banks, states, brokers, intermediaries. Increasingly, it is now administered by code, consensus, distributed systems. This is not merely technical; it is civilisational. It shifts the very definitions of ownership, exchange, and saving.

And yet, most newcomers are ushered into this world by speculation's side door. They are given a wallet and a dream, but not a map. They learn to buy without understanding why to hold. They memorise ticker codes before ever considering their own timelines. They stumble into ruin chasing someone else's playbook.

What you will find here is something else: context.

We will neither romanticise blockchain nor demonise it. We will look at it plainly—what it solves, where it fails, and how it redistributes trust. We will examine wallets not simply for their functions, but for what they signify. Because to hold your own keys is not just a technical act. It is a philosophical one. It declares whom you trust—and who you are becoming.

What does it mean to invest in crypto today? Not just the mechanics, but the mindset? That is the question this book pursues. For all its charts and code, crypto is deeply human—shaped as much by psychology as by engineering. People panic, overreach, pile in from FOMO and retreat in despair. They chase every new trend. They confuse action with wisdom. They trust the loudest voices while ignoring their own.

To navigate wisely, you must learn more than how to transact. You must learn how to see—with clarity, calm, and independence.

In the chapters ahead, you will be invited to interrogate the myths you may already carry—about wealth, speed, status, and success. You will be urged to define what a "good" crypto investment looks like for you—not in abstract ROI, but in terms aligned with your values, your horizon, your life. We will study the nuts and bolts—wallets, exchanges—but always through the lens of intention. Every password, every click, is a declaration about trust.

You will learn defence—not just against phishing emails, but against subtler dangers: the lure of convenience, the pull of conformity, the fog of confusion. You will see that safety is not a feature switch but a practice. That custody is not just a service but a culture. That wealth, when kept quietly and tended wisely, becomes a form of personal strength that requires no performance.

This is not a technical guide. Yet it will give you confidence with technical tools.
This is not a trading script. Yet you will emerge more strategic.
This is not a self-help book. Yet it will press on your inner landscape more than any market crash.

What we are building is an antifragile relationship with digital assets—one that strengthens in volatility. A stance rooted not in the fever of the market, but in the lucidity of your thought. If this sounds ambitious, it is only because the times demand it. The age of passive consumption is ending. In a decentralised world, you are no longer merely the customer. You are the bank. The custodian. The strategist. The risk officer.

The authority you have been seeking has been your own all along.

These chapters will equip you to shoulder that responsibility with calm and clarity. You will see that resisting hype is not only sensible but a first act of power. You will come to regard wallets as more than software—as declarations of sovereignty. You will learn how so-called "trustless" systems are built on intricate architectures of trust, and how to judge platforms not merely by output but by principle.

You will be challenged to stretch your sense of time—to think in decades, not in trading days. To invest with intention, not as if playing a game. To assemble a portfolio that reflects your reality, not some YouTube guru's. Along the way, you will face questions of privacy, taxation, and living across borders, and gain a clearer picture of what it means to invest globally yet live locally.

Above all, you will learn to see crypto not as a shortcut, but as a mirror.

If you have come to escape the noise, you are in the right place. If you arrived seeking the next hot tip, you may leave disappointed. But if your aim is to think deeply, act wisely, and build something that endures—not just materially but philosophically—this book is for you.

Let the markets rage. Let the hype spin itself dizzy. Here, we practise stillness. Here, the old virtues—patience, discipline, humility—are lifted again, under a new digital banner.

This is *The Quiet Ledger.* And it begins with you.

Chapter 1
Crypto Is Not a Shortcut—It's a Mirror

Crypto did not invent human folly, though it may well be the sharpest lens through which to observe it. The technology itself—elegant, decentralised, mathematical—operates with a kind of austere neutrality. It neither asks for your belief nor offers promises. Yet the culture surrounding it rarely mirrors this stillness. Instead, it is drenched in noise, volatility, and a relentless craving for whatever comes next. The dissonance is not accidental; it is baked into the structure. Crypto reflects back what we bring to it. Arrive with greed, and it magnifies that greed tenfold. Approach with fear, and every dip, every regulatory whisper, every cryptic tweet becomes an amplifier of dread. In this way, crypto is less marketplace than mirror—a mirror that throws into sharp relief the emotional undercurrents finance usually conceals.

To engage with crypto is, therefore, not simply to test-drive a new financial system. It is to confront ourselves, often in a rawer, heightened form. The volatility of coins and tokens is real enough, but its emotional twin is just as potent: the volatility of our own attention, desires, and identities. You can pore over charts for hours and still be undone by the psychological weight of holding through uncertainty—watching your holdings halve in a week, or resisting the itch to act when restraint is wiser. Crypto's deepest lessons are not encoded in its protocols but in the discipline it demands. The mirror does not flatter. It exposes.

The first distortion that mirror offers is hype. It saturates the air crypto breathes: YouTube thumbnails shouting "10x gains!", influencers peddling early retirement, Discord channels pulsing with breathless urgency. Hype is hardly unique—every technological shift has carried its own fever, from dot-com bubbles to gold rushes. But crypto's hype is peculiar in its velocity and reach. Information travels faster than comprehension. By the time a newcomer hears of a token, the "opportunity" has usually vanished—if it ever existed. And still the hype machine churns, powered less by truth than by raw emotion.

The sovereign investor's first act is to recognise hype for what it is: symptom, not signal. Hype reveals nothing of lasting value; it charts only the crowd's mood, swinging between frenzy and despair. The beginner's task is not to parse hype but to detach from it. Yet this is harder than it sounds. Hype bypasses intellect and seizes instinct. Its whisper is always the same: *Buy now, or miss it forever.* The antidote is not jaded cynicism but clarity. To remain grounded in a market designed to destabilise you is perhaps the rarest skill of all.

No surprise, then, that much of crypto's folklore revolves around the figure of the accidental millionaire. These are the stories that dazzle: the developer who mined Bitcoin in 2011 and forgot about it; the teenager who flipped a meme coin into six figures; the influencer who "made it" and now teaches others to do the same. They appeal because they promise a shortcut—wealth without grind, luck without labour. But such tales are not roadmaps. They are anomalies.

What those narratives omit is the survivor bias baked into every market. For each person who stumbled into riches, there are countless others who lost quietly—buying tops, holding too long, selling in despair, trusting the wrong protocol. Their stories never trend on Twitter. They are not quoted on podcasts. And yet their experiences are far more common. When we focus only on the dazzling few, our expectations warp. We begin to imagine that success is easy, sudden, random—when in reality it is deliberate, difficult, and slow.

That distortion is dangerous. It undermines the patience and discipline required to build durable positions. It seduces people into overexposure, into trusting shaky platforms, into trading on raw emotion. The myth of the accidental millionaire does not merely mislead—it actively damages. It plants the wrong lessons, grows the wrong mindset. If this book has a single mission, it is to dismantle that myth and replace it with something sturdier: sovereignty, clarity, realism.

Which raises a deeper question: when you say you *own* crypto, what exactly do you own?

It is astonishing how rarely this is asked. Most newcomers glance only at price, seeing their holdings as a number that rises or falls. But this lens is narrow, almost dangerously so. To own crypto is not merely financial—it is infrastructural. It is to participate in protocols, to shoulder responsibility for private keys, to navigate decentralised terrain, to accept a new relationship with custody and control. It is, in its truest sense, as political as it is financial.

At its most basic, ownership unfolds in three modes: speculation, utility, and sovereignty.

Speculation is the most common, and the least stable. Here crypto is a chip on the table, a ticket for flipping short-term gains. There is nothing inherently wrong with this, so long as it is named honestly: gambling with uncertain odds. It thrives on hype and withers in silence.

Utility sits on firmer ground. It treats crypto as a tool—accessing decentralised finance, interacting with smart contracts, transferring value across borders. Tokens here are not just stored but used. The risks lessen, but the complexity grows.

Sovereignty is the rarest and most mature. It is less about escape from fiat and more about responsibility. To self-custody is to say: *I am accountable for my assets.* To step into decentralised systems is to declare: *I place my trust in protocols over institutions.* Sovereignty is rarely easy, rarely convenient. But it coheres. It aligns with blockchain's deepest promises—autonomy, transparency, resilience.

The journey from speculation to sovereignty does not happen by accident. It usually requires unlearning, recalibration, sometimes loss. Many start with price and end with principle—only after hacks, scams, or heartbreak force a reckoning. Yet this evolution can also be chosen. It begins with a deceptively plain question: *What do I actually want from this?*

Which leads us to the matter of success.

Traditional finance measures success by numbers—returns, yields, percentages. Crypto demands something broader. It insists on emotional stamina, ethical clarity, and a horizon that stretches beyond this or that market cycle. Success might look like sleeping soundly through a 50% drawdown. It might mean safeguarding privacy in an economy built for surveillance. It might mean refusing to buy into a trending coin that collides with your values.

Success is not a figure on a chart. It is the alignment between your assets and your identity.

This chapter asks you to begin with the end in mind. Before you learn about wallets or exchanges or private keys, pause and ask: what would a successful relationship with crypto feel like? Would it mean peace of mind? Flexibility? A hedge against inflation? Participation in something larger than yourself? None of these answers is wrong. Only unexamined ones are dangerous. In a market this volatile, the most expensive liability is the assumption you never scrutinised.

By refusing hype, dismantling myths, clarifying ownership, and reimagining success, you set the stage for everything that follows. You begin not by acting but by seeing—your impulses, your habits, your blind spots. And in that seeing, you uncover crypto's most profound lesson: not how to outwit the market, but how to meet yourself.

Hype as a Symptom, Not a Signal

Step into the average crypto community, scroll through social media feeds, or glance at headlines during a bull run, and you'll encounter the same tone: urgency. The language is breathless. "Last chance." "This coin is about to explode." "Don't miss the next 100x." The sentiment is not just persuasive—it's coercive. Hype doesn't merely invite interest; it demands action. And yet, what's most striking is not the speed at which the market moves, but the speed at which *people react.*

The defining feature of crypto culture is not decentralisation, nor innovation, nor even volatility—it is *amplification.* Amplification of attention, of emotion, of behaviour. What would have once been a private curiosity becomes a global stampede in minutes. A rumour becomes a trading thesis. A tweet becomes a financial decision. This is not a sign of technological progress—it is a symptom of psychological unpreparedness. The true danger of hype is not that it distorts the market. It's that it distorts *us*.

Crypto functions as an accelerant. It takes the primal drives that have always animated markets—greed, fear, envy, euphoria—and places them in a new technological container: open 24/7, fuelled by frictionless access, and global in scale. This container has no natural cooling system. No pauses, no trading halts, no mandatory disclosures. The result is not simply a volatile asset class—it is a volatile *experience*.

And it's one that investors are rarely prepared for. Because most of us, when entering crypto, still carry an implicit assumption from traditional finance: that price signals information, that movement equals meaning, and that speed correlates with opportunity. In crypto, these associations quickly break down. Rapid price movement may be the result of nothing more than a celebrity endorsement, an algorithmic quirk, or a cascading liquidation. "Momentum" can be manufactured. "Fundamentals" may be irrelevant. And hype, more often than not, signals *nothing* about actual value. But it tells us volumes about collective psychology.

This misreading—confusing hype for signal—isn't just a tactical error. It's a philosophical one. It reflects a worldview in which the outer world is granted priority over the inner. We allow the market's mood to define our own. A price spike creates euphoria, regardless of context. A crash triggers despair, even if nothing substantive has changed. The volatility of the chart becomes a mirror of our own emotional volatility.

This is not a flaw in the market—it is a revelation. Crypto exposes our cognitive vulnerabilities not because it is flawed, but because it is *fast*. Its speed does not create emotion; it reveals it. And in doing so, it offers a rare opportunity: to observe ourselves in real time. To study our triggers. To notice the precise moment when curiosity becomes FOMO, when research becomes rationalisation, when risk tolerance becomes denial.

Resisting hype, then, is not merely an investment strategy. It is an act of self-governance. A refusal to be externally programmed. It means choosing clarity over momentum, principles over pressure. This is especially difficult because hype is social—it is experienced collectively. Being the one who does *not* rush in, who does *not* buy the trending token, who does *not* echo the dominant sentiment, often feels like dissonance. It is uncomfortable. But it is also the only way to cultivate sovereignty in a market designed to erode it.

Consider the 2017 ICO boom, when a torrent of white papers flooded the market, each promising to "disrupt" a particular industry. Billions were raised. Many projects vanished. A handful pivoted. Very few delivered. The hype, in hindsight, was an echo chamber. Promoters cited each other, investors justified bets with borrowed conviction, and due diligence was reduced to little more than fear of missing out. What was missing wasn't intelligence—it was *discernment*. The ability to say: this is exciting, but is it real? Is it necessary? Is it sustainable?

This pattern repeated itself with NFTs in 2021. Projects launched with high-profile drops, viral marketing, and instant resale markets. "Community" became a euphemism for speculative coordination. Floor prices became proxies for cultural relevance. And yet, behind many of these projects were hastily assembled teams, vague roadmaps, and no clear utility. Again, the hype was overwhelming. But it wasn't a signal. It was a symptom—of scarcity narratives, of speculative fatigue, of the psychological pressure to *not* be left behind.

The problem with hype isn't just that it misleads. It's that it *distracts*. It pulls attention away from the slow, patient work of understanding a technology, assessing a project's fundamentals, evaluating trade-offs, and aligning with personal investment goals. In the presence of hype, nuance dies. The complexity of protocol design, the ethics of decentralisation, the implications of tokenomics—these are flattened into slogans. "Going to the moon." "WAGMI." "This is the future." Such phrases don't explain—they sedate.

To be immune to hype is not to be indifferent. It is to observe without being absorbed. It is to read a white paper without checking the market cap. To attend a Twitter Space without adjusting your portfolio mid-sentence. To recognise that some of the best opportunities in crypto will not be trending—because they are boring, underreported, or still in gestation. They are not loud. And they don't need to be.

There's a deeper layer still. Hype, at its core, often appeals to our desire for simplicity in the face of complexity. The crypto ecosystem is vast, fast-moving, and often opaque. It's tempting to collapse that complexity into a single narrative: "This is the next Bitcoin." "This will replace Ethereum." "This coin solves everything." But reductionism is not clarity—it's an escape from the labour of thinking. And the danger of hype is not merely that we follow the crowd, but that we *abdicate responsibility* for understanding what we own, why we own it, and what risks we are taking.

To push back against hype is to reassert intellectual agency. It's to say: I will not outsource my conviction. I will not conflate market excitement with truth. I will not confuse volatility with importance. This is not a call for cynicism, but for maturity. To be sceptical is not to reject innovation—it is to honour it by taking it seriously.

The discipline of resisting hype also cultivates a quality that is radically undervalued in the crypto world: patience. The ability to *not act* when others do. The ability to wait, observe, and evaluate. Patience is not passive. It is active restraint. It is a refusal to be timed by someone else's clock. And it is, perhaps, the rarest asset in a space where immediacy is the dominant currency.

This restraint is not without reward. The investor who avoids hype cycles is less likely to be overexposed to vaporware, less vulnerable to rug pulls, and less emotionally compromised by market swings. But the deeper reward is psychological. By observing one's own reactions to hype—without immediately acting on them—one becomes more self-aware. And self-awareness is the foundation of all good decision-making.

There are, of course, exceptions. Moments when real breakthroughs attract real excitement. Bitcoin's early traction was not hype—it was history. Ethereum's rollout of smart contracts changed the game. But even in these moments, the noise that followed often outpaced the signal. The key is not to reject all enthusiasm, but to differentiate between *earned excitement* and *engineered urgency*.

So how does one practically resist hype?

Not through isolation, but through intentional exposure. Curate your inputs. Seek voices who are willing to say "I don't know." Study projects slowly, across market cycles. Hold fewer assets with more conviction. Ask uncomfortable questions. What does this token *actually* do? Who benefits from its adoption? What are the risks? What am I assuming? And perhaps most critically: *Would I still own this if no one else was talking about it?*

These questions don't inoculate you against all mistakes. But they shift your posture from reactive to reflective. From externally driven to internally anchored. And that is the posture of a sovereign investor.

Crypto will always attract hype. It is an industry built on imagination and disruption. But imagination without discernment becomes delusion. And disruption without integrity becomes destruction. If crypto is to fulfil its deeper promises—of open systems, programmable trust, and individual empowerment—it must be stewarded by participants who are not merely excited, but *clear*. Participants who can see the mirror, and recognise the reflection.

Hype is loud. But clarity is quiet. The latter takes longer to cultivate—but it lasts longer too. And in a market where everything moves fast, perhaps the most radical act is to move slowly. To think carefully. To wait until your reasons for investing are stronger than the noise telling you to act.

Because in the end, the market is not your master. It is your mirror. And what you see in it is not just the price of coins—but the cost of being unprepared.

The Myth of the Accidental Millionaire

The story is always the same. A young coder stumbles upon Bitcoin in its infancy, mines a few hundred for fun, and forgets about them. Years later, they remember the stash, recover the keys, and discover they're sitting on millions. Or a university student hears about a joke token in a meme forum, throws in £200, and by sheer timing watches it balloon into a life-changing windfall. These tales are told and retold, always with the same arc: ignorance or indifference rewarded by extreme luck. They have become the modern fairytales of the digital economy. But unlike folklore, which often contains moral instruction beneath the fantasy, these stories mislead by omission. They seduce with spectacle and leave out everything that makes wealth sustainable, repeatable, or earned.

The myth of the accidental millionaire is not simply inaccurate—it's corrosive. It distorts expectations, incentivises recklessness, and undermines the deliberate, disciplined practices that form the bedrock of sound investing. It reframes luck as strategy and timing as insight. And in doing so, it creates an environment in which serious investors—especially beginners—are constantly measuring their progress against a fiction. The damage isn't just financial. It's psychological. Because when success appears random, the investor either chases it blindly or disengages entirely, concluding that the rules don't matter because the game is rigged.

This mythology thrives in crypto more than in any other sector for one reason: *visibility*. Traditional markets rarely televise their extremes. You don't often see TikToks of pension funds growing modestly over thirty years. But in crypto, platforms like X, Reddit, and YouTube amplify the exceptions. The person who turned £500 into £2 million is front-page news. The thousands who lost the same amount chasing similar promises vanish into statistical silence. This imbalance of narrative is a textbook case of *survivor bias*—a cognitive distortion where we focus only on the winners and ignore the vast field of losses buried behind them.

Consider the 2021 bull run. Amid the euphoria, social media was flooded with screenshots of extraordinary gains—wallet balances, before-and-after stories, charts showing meteoric rises. These posts were not instructional; they were performative. They did not teach strategy, analysis, or risk management. They taught envy, urgency, and belief in miracles. The unspoken message: "This could be you." For many, that was all it took to jump in, often late, often unprepared. When the inevitable correction came, the winners went quiet. The losses, however, remained.

These stories of sudden wealth create a dangerous incentive structure. They reward impulsivity. They romanticise ignorance. They frame minimal research as a virtue—an implication that overthinking is counterproductive, and that analysis somehow gets in the way of big wins. It's a worldview in which diligence is boring and caution is a liability. The result is a culture in which serious research is undervalued and reckless gambling is misbranded as bold investing.

The truth is, there is no consistent pattern of behaviour that leads to accidental wealth. There is only *retrospective narrative*. Someone may have gotten lucky with an obscure altcoin, but that doesn't make buying random tokens a replicable strategy. There's a profound difference between a *repeatable process* and a *lucky event*. Conflating the two is not just intellectually lazy—it's dangerous.

Survivor bias also extends beyond individuals to entire market cycles. Projects that succeeded are often studied with the benefit of hindsight clarity, while those that failed are forgotten entirely. Ethereum is praised for its longevity and network effects, but few remember the dozens of smart contract platforms that launched around the same time with similar rhetoric and collapsed in obscurity. When we study only what worked, we develop distorted models of what success requires. We overlook timing, network externalities, regulatory context, and sheer randomness.

There is also a subtler danger embedded in the accidental millionaire myth: the idea that *the earlier you enter, the more you deserve.* This narrative implies a kind of moral seniority based on timing, not contribution. It equates proximity to origin with insight, when in fact early entrants are just as prone to error, tribalism, and hype as anyone else. Some made fortunes because they understood the tech and its implications. Others simply happened to be present. We must be able to tell the difference. Otherwise, we elevate luck into wisdom, and confuse temporal advantage with philosophical clarity.

This has implications for how newcomers are mentored—or, more accurately, misled. In online spaces, veterans who profited from early investments are often granted de facto authority. But being early is not a credential. The ability to teach, to analyse, to adapt through multiple cycles—*that* is what makes someone worth listening to. Yet in a culture obsessed with net worth over knowledge, wealth alone becomes the arbiter of truth. This is a distortion not just of investing principles, but of epistemology. It replaces earned insight with anecdotal dominance.

There are, of course, legitimate paths to wealth in crypto. People who studied cryptography, who understood monetary theory, who learned how to evaluate code, who tracked developer activity, who saw emerging consensus mechanisms and interpreted their implications—many of these individuals acted with conviction before the market did. But their success was not random. It was informed. And it did not happen overnight. The difference between these individuals and the mythologised millionaire is stark. One is a practitioner. The other is a story.

The accidental millionaire myth also distorts our tolerance for time. Investing—when done well—is a long, often boring process. It involves waiting, reassessing, enduring drawdowns, holding through boredom, and resisting the urge to pivot constantly. The myth makes all of that feel unnecessary. Why wait when someone else got rich in a week? Why study fundamentals when a friend doubled their investment by chance? This psychological pressure corrodes the investor's timeline. It creates a mismatch between *expectation* and *reality*. And when reality fails to deliver instant returns, frustration sets in—not because the strategy was flawed, but because the timeframe was warped.

This dissonance is compounded by media. Financial journalism, driven by clicks and attention, often centres on extreme outcomes. Long-term wealth accumulation is difficult to narrate. But sensational wins? Those stories write themselves. The result is an informational environment that overrepresents luck and underrepresents discipline. For the thoughtful investor, this creates a challenge: to filter noise from signal, to look past virality and toward viability.

To build a healthy mindset in crypto—or any market—you must disarm the narrative of instant success. Replace the fantasy with process. Replace urgency with inquiry. Replace envy with rigour. Ask yourself: What is the investment thesis? What problem does this protocol solve? What are the risks? Who benefits if this succeeds—and who bears the downside if it fails? These questions anchor you in reality. They make it possible to distinguish between speculation and conviction.

There is also a profound ethical dimension to consider. The celebration of accidental millionaires implies a zero-sum logic: that your gain is someone else's loss, and that wealth is a matter of timing, not value creation. This is the opposite of sustainable finance. It encourages extractive behaviour. It turns investing into opportunism, and markets into casinos. If crypto is to realise its deeper promise—a more open, decentralised, and equitable financial architecture—it cannot be built on narratives of luck. It must be built on understanding.

Resisting the myth of the accidental millionaire is more than a matter of personal discipline. It is a matter of collective maturity. It means telling better stories—ones that reflect effort, curiosity, prudence, and resilience. It means highlighting those who built slowly and well, not just those who struck gold. It means building a culture in which success is measured not by speed, but by alignment between capital and conscience.

Crypto's early history will always be punctuated by dramatic fortunes. That is inevitable in any new frontier. But for this ecosystem to mature—for it to become more than just a speculative theatre—it needs more than winners. It needs stewards. It needs people who are not impressed by overnight wealth, but by sustained clarity. People who ask *not* "How much did you make?" but "How well did you understand what you were doing?"

That is the investor worth becoming. Not the one who got lucky once. But the one who can make informed decisions, again and again, under changing conditions, with steady hands and clear eyes. The one who does not need hype, or myth, or miracles. Just method, patience, and integrity.

What You Actually Own When You Own Crypto

Most people think they're buying coins. They see a digital asset listed on an exchange, enter a position, and watch numbers shift on a screen. But this surface-level transaction obscures a more profound question—one few investors pause to consider: *What exactly do I own when I own crypto?* The answer is not merely technical. It is architectural, psychological, and, in the deepest sense, existential.

Because to own crypto is not just to hold an asset. It is to make a wager on a radically different system of trust, control, and self-responsibility. It is to reconfigure one's place in the financial order.

The prevailing confusion around ownership stems from a cultural misalignment. Most people come to crypto from legacy financial systems. In those systems, ownership is custodial. You own a stock, but it's held by a brokerage. You have a bank account, but the bank holds the money. You interact through interfaces—apps, platforms, passwords—but rarely do you control the infrastructure. Value is always mediated. There's always someone else in the room. Crypto, by contrast, offers a type of ownership that is direct, disintermediated, and final. But with that freedom comes a new kind of exposure. When you own crypto, especially self-custodied crypto, *there is no fallback*. You are the custodian. You are the interface. You are the authority.

But that technical clarity belies a deeper complexity. Because not all ownership is created equal. There is a profound difference between *speculative*, *utilitarian*, and *sovereign* ownership. These categories are not mutually exclusive, but they do reflect distinct mindsets—and they lead to radically different behaviours.

Speculative ownership is the most common, especially among new entrants. It treats crypto as a volatile asset class, a financial instrument whose only purpose is to appreciate in price. The holder of speculative crypto typically focuses on charts, trends, and narratives. The asset is a number, and its only meaningful attribute is whether that number is rising or falling. In this framework, the blockchain doesn't matter. The protocol's purpose is irrelevant. Tokenomics are skimmed over. The token is a ticket—its intrinsic properties matter less than its perceived market momentum. This kind of ownership is inherently unstable, not only in market terms but in emotional ones. It is reactive, driven by sentiment and peer influence. The asset is disposable. If the price drops, the belief drops with it.

Speculation has always existed in markets, and it serves a function: it brings liquidity, attention, and early capital. But it is a shallow form of engagement. It doesn't confer resilience. When markets correct, speculative holders tend to exit first. Not because they lack capital—but because they lack conviction. They never really *understood* what they held in the first place. It was never theirs in any meaningful sense.

Utilitarian ownership is more grounded. It arises when an asset has a function beyond price movement. This includes using Ethereum to pay for gas, staking tokens in a DeFi protocol, participating in a DAO, or interacting with NFTs that grant access, identity, or rights. In these cases, the asset is a tool. It facilitates participation. It does something. This kind of ownership is more aligned with the ethos of decentralised systems. It requires literacy—understanding how wallets work, how smart contracts execute, what permissions are being granted. Utility binds the owner to the ecosystem. There is a purpose to the holding that goes beyond exit strategies.

But utility alone does not confer sovereignty. One can use a product without controlling it. And that's where the third and most profound form of ownership emerges: *sovereign ownership.* This is where the philosophical gravity of crypto begins to assert itself. Sovereign ownership is not just about what you *have*—it's about what you *assume responsibility for.* It is the act of holding your own keys. Of verifying transactions. Of choosing protocols based on values, not just yield. It is the conscious decision to hold assets in a way that *cannot* be reversed by a third party. To own crypto sovereignly is to exit the mental framework of dependence. It is not merely financial; it is a form of digital self-possession.

This shift is not trivial. It requires the investor to confront a new set of risks: What if I lose my seed phrase? What if I make a mistake? What if I become my own weakest link? These are legitimate fears—but they are also the necessary growing pains of digital maturity. In sovereign ownership, *risk is not eliminated; it is relocated.* The platform no longer holds the liability—you do. The transaction no longer requires permission—you provide it. This is not freedom in the casual sense. It is freedom with consequence. And that is the essence of sovereignty.

This distinction—between speculative, utilitarian, and sovereign holding—is more than semantic. It shapes everything from security practices to time horizons to emotional behaviour. A speculative investor checks prices daily. A sovereign investor may not check for weeks. The former is tethered to market sentiment. The latter is tethered to principle. One acts when provoked. The other acts when ready.

This also reconfigures the question of value. If value is defined purely in price terms, then a token is only as good as its current market price. But if value includes *function*, *resilience*, and *alignment with one's worldview*, then some assets may be undervalued in conventional terms but deeply valuable in personal or ideological ones. For instance, holding Bitcoin not as a hedge but as a form of civil resistance—against inflation, surveillance, or capital controls—is not a financial bet; it's a declaration. The value is not in what the coin does today, but in what it *represents* over time.

To own crypto, in this more expansive frame, is to participate in a shift in economic architecture. You are not just holding a digital coin. You are holding an idea—about how money should work, who should control it, and what mechanisms should govern trust. That's what makes this space so complex. It's not just technical; it's ideological. And ownership becomes a way of signalling not only where you want to store your value, but how you understand the concept of *value* itself.

It's worth pausing to consider what's really being decentralised here. Not just the storage of data or the verification of transactions—but the very foundations of custodianship, access, and identity. In legacy systems, ownership is often a matter of account permissions. Your bank account is owned in name, but its use is governed by terms, policies, and often, institutional discretion. In decentralised systems, ownership is not a matter of permission—it is a matter of possession. The phrase "not your keys, not your coins" is more than a slogan. It is a structural truth.

But this autonomy comes with weight. True ownership means you are no longer shielded by the familiar guardrails. There is no help desk, no reversible transaction, no "forgot password" link. This forces a reevaluation not only of how we handle digital assets, but of how we handle *ourselves*. Are we ready to take full responsibility for our digital life? Do we have the attention span, the discipline, the situational awareness to manage irreversible control?

This is why crypto ownership is, at its core, existential. Because it asks not just what you want to hold, but *how* you want to live. It invites reflection on autonomy, risk, patience, and long-term thinking. It challenges default settings inherited from a lifetime of convenience-based finance. And it offers a stark but empowering message: *You can have more control, but you must first become someone who can wield it.*

That, ultimately, is the philosophical heart of crypto—not as a speculative playground, but as a proving ground for sovereignty. To own well in this space is to take full responsibility for your actions, your security, your thinking, and your future. It is to decline the comfort of delegation in favour of the discipline of independence. It is to see that every wallet is a mirror, every transaction a choice, and every holding a position not just on markets, but on meaning.

You do not merely own coins. You own agency. You own exposure. You own the outcomes—good or bad—not because someone else decided them, but because you did. That is what ownership means in crypto. Not passive possession, but active presence. Not financial convenience, but philosophical clarity. And in a world of increasing abstraction, that may be the most tangible thing of all.

Begin With the End: What Does Success Really Look Like?

If you can't define success, someone else will define it for you. And in the world of crypto, that definition is almost always financial. Success is framed as numerical: net worth, percentage gain, early entry, fortunate exits. The ticker becomes the barometer of intelligence. But this is a fragile architecture on which to build one's relationship to digital assets. Because markets are unstable, prices are volatile, and financial milestones—once reached—rarely bring the clarity or contentment they promised. The moment you hit one, another appears. A higher goal, a larger number, a more exclusive benchmark. This endless escalation hollows out the process, turning investing into a kind of financial performance art. The question isn't just what you want from crypto. It's what you'll count as *enough*—and why.

That's why this chapter begins not with tactics, but with purpose. Before you study wallets or exchanges or protocols, before you learn the mechanics of decentralised finance or the distinctions between blockchains, you must pause and ask: *What would a meaningful outcome look like for me?* Not in someone else's language. Not in social metrics. In yours. Because crypto, unlike traditional finance, does not come preloaded with a social contract. There's no consensus about what success looks like here. That is both its risk and its opportunity. You can define success in your own terms—but only if you do it deliberately.

There's a tendency, especially among new entrants, to mirror the goals of the loudest voices in the space. Some aim for financial independence. Others for status in a niche community. Still others want to fund open-source projects, or simply hedge against traditional finance. But these motivations are rarely interrogated. They're absorbed by osmosis—picked up from Discord chats, YouTube channels, and anecdotal success stories. This is how investors end up pursuing goals they don't actually believe in, chasing numbers they didn't originally care about, and behaving in ways they later regret.

The remedy is clarity. Not just intellectual clarity, but ethical and emotional clarity. Success must be understood not as a destination, but as a set of internal conditions: *How do I want to feel while investing? What do I want to be true about my behaviour under pressure? What do I want to walk away from this process having preserved or developed—not just financially, but personally?*

This reframing is not indulgent—it's essential. Because investing is not just the act of allocating capital. It is the act of allocating attention, time, and identity. The decisions you make—what to buy, when to hold, how to respond to a crash—are expressions of your values, whether you realise it or not. And without a stable internal definition of success, the volatility of external markets will drag you into emotional extremes. You'll oscillate between euphoria and anxiety, not because the asset has changed, but because you never decided what you were aiming for in the first place.

This becomes particularly acute in bear markets. When prices fall and hype dissipates, investors without a clear internal compass tend to panic or disengage. Those with a well-articulated purpose, however, are more likely to remain grounded. They can evaluate a downtrend not as a failure, but as a phase. They don't define themselves by temporary conditions because their definition of success was never contingent on short-term price movement.

This mindset also transforms how you assess risk. Without a clear endpoint, risk is always framed as financial loss. But when success is measured in emotional or ethical terms, risk becomes more complex. Losing money might be acceptable if it was done in line with your principles. Preserving capital might be a form of failure if it required constant anxiety or compromised your values. A portfolio that doubles in value but robs you of peace is not a success—it's a cost.

Success, then, should be evaluated across three axes: *emotional*, *ethical*, and *temporal*.

Emotionally, what does stability look like for you? Are you able to hold through drawdowns without losing sleep? Do your decisions reflect calm observation or reactive impulse? Emotional success means being able to stay with your strategy even when the market is screaming. It means designing your approach in such a way that you don't constantly second-guess yourself, because you've already accounted for volatility in your expectations.

Ethically, are your investments aligned with your deeper principles? This can mean many things: avoiding projects with extractive tokenomics, choosing to support protocols that prioritise transparency, or simply refusing to profit from platforms that rely on manipulation or unsustainable incentives. Crypto provides the unique ability to opt into systems with very different value architectures. Success, from an ethical lens, may mean participating only in networks you believe improve the world—even if that limits your upside.

Temporally, what is your horizon? Are you investing with a five-year vision? A ten-year thesis? Or are you trying to maximise this quarter's gains? Temporal clarity shapes everything: what you hold, how you allocate, and how you react to news. Without it, you will be perpetually vulnerable to short-term noise. But when your horizon is long enough, most fluctuations become irrelevant. You stop trying to "time" the market, and start trying to *understand* it.

Defining success across these three dimensions has another benefit: it helps you resist mimicry. In crypto, it is dangerously easy to adopt someone else's conviction. You see a portfolio allocation that worked for them, and you copy it. You hear a thesis that resonates emotionally, and you adopt it without pressure testing. But mimicry is brittle. It doesn't survive stress. When the market turns, you'll abandon a borrowed thesis far more quickly than one you've reasoned through yourself. True success is not just about outcomes—it's about authorship. Did you make the decision, or did you just follow?

This brings us to the concept of *autobiographical investing*—the idea that your portfolio should reflect your actual life, not someone else's ambition. Are you a parent with limited time to monitor markets? Then strategies that require constant engagement are probably misaligned. Are you a technologist who understands the infrastructure deeply? Then your edge may lie in long-tail protocols others overlook. Are you operating under regulatory constraints in your jurisdiction? That should shape how you engage with staking, privacy coins, or decentralised exchanges. Investing is not abstract—it is lived. And the closer your strategy maps to your life, the more sustainable it becomes.

It's also worth acknowledging the tension between ambition and realism. There is a strain of thinking in crypto that treats modest goals as unambitious. If you're not trying to 10x your capital, are you even playing the game? This is toxic. It assumes that the only reason to invest is to escape, to break out, to dramatically transform one's socioeconomic status. But many of the healthiest investors are not trying to escape anything. They're building buffers. They're cultivating optionality. They're increasing their agency—not because they hate their lives, but because they want to protect what matters.

This is where the real shift occurs: when you stop asking *How much can I gain?* and start asking *What kind of person do I want to be while gaining it?* Success becomes less about magnitude and more about integrity. The amount matters, but only in context. £10,000 earned through consistent, values-aligned behaviour may be more meaningful than £100,000 gained through constant stress, compromise, or borrowed conviction. The metric shifts from ROI to *ROE*: return on effort, on emotion, on ethics.

A well-defined concept of success also protects against the tyranny of comparison. In a space where everyone seems to be outperforming, it's easy to feel inadequate. But when your success criteria are internally defined, you stop measuring yourself against someone else's highlights. You don't feel behind because you're on your own track. This doesn't make you complacent—it makes you coherent.

Eventually, this mindset becomes the foundation for all technical learning. You don't study security practices just to avoid loss; you study them because they protect what matters to you. You don't explore new protocols just for yield; you explore them because they may align better with your values or your time horizon. Strategy becomes integrated with identity. Every technical decision is contextualised by personal meaning.

And that's the ultimate goal. Not just to make informed decisions, but to make *your* decisions. To hold assets that reflect your principles. To tolerate volatility because you've already decided what it means—and what it doesn't. To walk away from hype because you know what you're aiming for. To succeed not because you guessed right, but because you thought clearly.

Begin with the end. Not because the end is fixed, but because *having one* will change everything that follows.

Chapter 2
The Architecture of Trust in a Trustless System

Every meaningful financial system rests on an invisible but indispensable foundation: trust. Trust that your balance will remain intact overnight. Trust that the institution safeguarding your funds will neither collapse nor confiscate them. Trust that ledgers are accurate, intermediaries honest, and the wider system resilient. For centuries, this trust has been institutional—anchored in the authority of banks, governments, and legal frameworks. Yet institutions are fallible: slow to adapt, open to political interference, opaque by nature, and often aligned with interests far removed from those of the individuals they claim to serve. The most radical promise of crypto is not the digitisation of money, but the redistribution of trust itself—from hierarchical structures to decentralised protocols, from human discretion to machine consensus.

To grasp this transition is to see what blockchain technology truly represents—and, equally, what it does not. Crypto does not abolish trust; it rearranges it. Instead of vesting confidence in a central actor, trust is encoded into rules, consensus mechanisms, and distributed networks. Yet this is not a neat exchange of one form of trust for another. It is a tangled trade-off. The faith once placed in institutions is now spread across software, validators, community governance, cryptographic primitives, and the vigilance of users themselves. In moving from institutions to protocols, trust has not disappeared—it has become more plural, more technical, and decidedly more personal.

This shift makes little sense without a glance backwards. Traditional finance revolved around central authorities because large-scale coordination demanded it. Before the internet, there was no alternative for managing ledgers, enforcing contracts, or resolving disputes. Trust was not just a social virtue; it was infrastructural necessity. Banks, courts, notaries, regulators—these were the trust factories of the industrial era. Their authority was reinforced by physical branches, legal codes, and institutional memory. You walked into a branch, shook hands with a manager, signed a paper. You trusted because you could point to someone—or something—tangible.

Blockchain replaces that concrete trust with probabilistic assurance. Its confidence emerges not from authority but from consensus. Multiple nodes verify each transaction independently. Once recorded, data becomes effectively immutable. There is no single point of failure, no gatekeeper, no database subject to unilateral tampering. Its architecture is adversarial at the root: it assumes bad actors will appear and hardens itself accordingly. That is a profound departure from traditional finance, which assumes good behaviour and punishes exceptions. In crypto, mistrust is not a flaw; it is a design principle.

Still, to collapse this reality into slogans—"trustless," "immutable," "decentralised"—is to lose nuance. No system is truly trustless. Blockchains still depend on trust: trust in the correctness of code, in validator honesty, in governance mechanisms, in the network's ongoing participation. Code may execute predictably, but code is written and updated by humans. And humans, as history never tires of reminding us, are prone to error.

The lesson has already been lived. The DAO hack of 2016, for example, exploited a vulnerability in a smart contract, siphoning millions in ETH. The Ethereum community responded with a fork, reversing the damage. This was not code at work, but politics. Consensus was social as well as algorithmic. If code alone were law, the hack would have stood. Instead, the community asserted authority, exposing the limits of "trustless" rhetoric. Protocols cannot banish politics. They merely relocate it.

This brings us to an uncomfortable truth: while blockchains remove central authorities, they do not abolish authority altogether. They distribute it. The question shifts from *Who controls this system?* to *How is control distributed, and can that distribution be manipulated?* In proof-of-stake systems, for instance, influence correlates with stake, often leading to power concentration among early adopters or large holders. In proof-of-work systems, mining centralisation remains an enduring concern, with a handful of pools wielding disproportionate control. These are not rare anomalies—they are structural patterns. And they deserve scrutiny.

As a result, trust in crypto becomes strikingly technical. Investors are compelled to ask what once only engineers pondered: Has this protocol been audited? Are incentives aligned? Is the validator set genuinely decentralised? Who controls upgrades, and through what mechanism? These are not academic curiosities. They determine whether your assets are genuinely secure—or merely appear to be.

Here another point emerges: perfect security does not exist. No system, centralised or decentralised, is immune to failure. Yet crypto's language often implies otherwise. Words like "unhackable," "immutable," and "censorship-resistant" carry an air of absoluteness. In truth, they are probabilistic. Immutability holds so long as consensus persists. Censorship resistance depends on geographic and political diversity. Even private keys—the very symbol of user control—are only as safe as the habits of the person guarding them.

And here lies the paradox: in trying to remove trust, crypto places more weight on the individual than ever. It is "trustless" only in that you need not trust others. But you must trust yourself—your memory, your operational discipline, your ability to secure backups, avoid phishing, and identify legitimate software. Failures here are not rare accidents; they are common hazards. Lost keys, compromised wallets, malicious dApps—these are not fringe risks, but central ones.

So what, then, is the architecture of trust in a supposedly trustless world?

It is not a monolith but a mosaic. It stretches across cryptography and social consensus, across network design and human governance. It resides in developer integrity and user vigilance alike. It is shaped by incentives, game theory, cultural norms, and user interfaces. Trust in crypto is neither wholly technological nor wholly social—it is both, intertwined. And unless you understand this layered complexity, your investments risk being guided more by speculation than clarity.

You are not merely purchasing tokens. You are entering systems of trust. Systems that encode certain values, exclude others, reward specific behaviours, and penalise alternatives. Systems that can be forked, captured, strengthened, or abandoned. Each protocol carries its own trust architecture—its own weave of risks, incentives, and coordination mechanisms. To invest wisely is to look beneath the market cap and ask: What assumptions about human behaviour underpin this system? Are those assumptions credible? Who holds influence, and how might that change under stress?

These are not just technical enquiries. They are philosophical, civic, and deeply human. For crypto is not merely a financial experiment; it is a reconsideration of how people coordinate, transact, and enforce commitments in a digital age. At its core lies one stubborn truth: you are not outside the system—you are part of it. Your choices—what you hold, what you support, what you secure, how you vote—shape its trajectory.

To operate in a "trustless" environment is not to escape trust, but to choose where and how it is placed. It is a shift from passive reliance to active responsibility. It demands not blind faith in code, but informed, ongoing discernment.

This chapter will not hand out simplistic answers. Instead, it will offer questions worth holding, frameworks for analysis, and tools for scrutiny. We will consider what blockchains solve—and what they leave unsolved. We will examine how human judgement threads itself through even the most decentralised structures. We will study how security is constructed, rather than assumed. And we will map how trust—once concentrated in a few global institutions—has been cracked apart, redistributed, and reassembled in fragile, evolving forms.

Crypto does not erase trust. It remixes it. To understand that remix—what it enables, what it risks, what it asks of you—is to step beyond speculation into sovereignty. That is the foundation of true investing: not hype, not hope, but structural awareness. Trust, examined.

From Institutions to Protocols: A Historic Shift

Trust has always been the cornerstone of economic coordination. Without trust, markets falter, credit collapses, and commerce reverts to barter. But the *location* of trust—where it is placed, how it is enforced, and who controls it—has changed profoundly over time. For centuries, the centralisation of trust in financial institutions was both a technological necessity and a social norm. Banks, governments, clearinghouses, and auditors evolved not just as service providers, but as the infrastructure of belief. They were the intermediaries of certainty. Yet in recent decades, this structure has been called into question—first by the fragility of centralised systems, and now by the emergence of a new paradigm: decentralised protocols.

The transition from institutions to protocols is not merely a shift in tools or techniques. It is a structural rethinking of how economic coordination is achieved. Traditional finance relies on top-down enforcement. Contracts are valid because courts say they are. Transactions are final because a central ledger says so. Access is determined by compliance with an institution's rules, often opaque, subject to interpretation, and enforced through bureaucratic gatekeeping. In contrast, decentralised finance replaces these trust anchors with code. Smart contracts execute agreements automatically. Distributed ledgers validate ownership collectively. Access becomes a matter of cryptographic authentication, not institutional permission.

To grasp the magnitude of this transition, it's necessary to understand *why* institutions became so central in the first place. In pre-modern societies, economic coordination was hyperlocal. Trust operated within communities, face-to-face, reinforced by social ties and reputation. But as commerce scaled—across empires, continents, and eventually into digital space—this informal trust proved insufficient. Institutions emerged to manage risk and enforce reliability at scale. Banks handled custody. Courts settled disputes.

Central banks stabilised currency. These were not optional features of financial life; they were the sinews holding it together.

This system worked—until it didn't. Crises like the 2008 financial meltdown revealed the costs of institutional opacity and moral hazard. When trust is concentrated, its failure is catastrophic. The fallout from one institution's collapse ripples across systems. Moreover, the institutional model embeds asymmetries of power. Customers are often subject to arbitrary restrictions, surveillance, or exclusion. Global inequality is compounded by uneven access to stable currencies, functional legal systems, or reliable banking infrastructure. For billions of people, the problem isn't too little innovation—it's too much dependence on systems they neither chose nor control.

Into this void stepped a new proposition: what if trust could be *distributed*? What if, instead of trusting a single institution, one could trust a protocol—transparent, predictable, and open to anyone who could interact with it? This is the foundational idea behind blockchain technology. Bitcoin, the first and still most iconic example, did not just introduce a digital currency. It introduced a new trust model. Transactions were verified not by a bank, but by a decentralised network of nodes. The ledger was not private, but public. The rules were not enforced by lawyers, but by consensus algorithms and cryptographic proofs.

Ethereum expanded this idea further, turning the blockchain into a programmable platform. Now, not just currency, but *contracts* could be decentralised. Lending, borrowing, trading, even governance—all could be reimagined as software, enforced not by courts but by code. This wasn't just a technical innovation. It was a shift in how trust is conceived and distributed.

But this shift is not without trade-offs. Protocols solve some trust problems by creating others. The removal of intermediaries reduces points of failure—but also removes safety nets. If a bank makes a mistake, you can call someone. If you send crypto to the wrong address, the transaction is irreversible. If a smart contract contains a bug, it may execute that bug precisely as written, draining funds with perfect efficiency. The protocol does not know what you *meant*—only what the code allows. The rigidity that makes decentralised systems trustworthy also makes them unforgiving.

Moreover, decentralisation itself is a spectrum, not a binary. Many protocols that advertise themselves as "trustless" still contain centralised choke points: admin keys that allow developers to pause contracts, governance processes controlled by a small number of token holders, oracles that feed external data into the system and can be compromised. These elements introduce re-centralisation under new names. Trust is not removed—it is *rearranged.* It migrates from visible institutions to hidden dependencies.

This requires a new literacy. Users must now understand not just the user interface, but the underlying trust architecture. Who runs the nodes? Who controls the upgrade process? What happens if the protocol forks? These are not theoretical concerns. They shape the security, longevity, and neutrality of the system. A decentralised exchange may operate without intermediaries, but if its liquidity is bootstrapped by a handful of providers, its market depth can vanish under stress. A lending protocol may be governed by token holders, but if governance participation is minimal, decisions can be hijacked by a minority.

Critically, these questions cannot be answered solely by code. Every protocol is embedded in a human context. Developers make choices. Communities interpret outcomes. Users vote, fork, or flee. Even the most elegant protocol depends on active maintenance, collective buy-in, and evolving norms. The notion that blockchain eliminates trust is not just incorrect—it's conceptually incoherent. What blockchain *does* is make trust more visible, more programmable, and more distributed. The question is no longer whether trust exists, but *where it resides and how it is enacted.*

Consider the case of MakerDAO, one of the earliest and most influential decentralised finance protocols. At its core, Maker allows users to generate a stablecoin, DAI, by locking up collateral. The rules governing how much collateral is required, what assets are accepted, and how risk is managed are encoded in smart contracts—but those contracts are adjustable through a system of on-chain governance. Token holders propose and vote on changes. This sounds democratic, but in practice, participation has often been low, and a small number of actors wield disproportionate influence. The protocol works, but it requires ongoing scrutiny—not just of the codebase, but of the political economy it creates.

This leads to a deeper point. Every protocol is a constitution in miniature. It defines who can do what, under what conditions, and with what consequences. But unlike traditional constitutions, protocols are enforced automatically. They leave little room for interpretation, discretion, or mercy. This gives them strength—but also brittleness. When conditions change, when edge cases emerge, when something breaks, the protocol does not adapt on its own. Humans must intervene. The myth of the "trustless" system is that it operates in isolation. In reality, it is embedded in—and dependent upon—a social substrate.

That's why trust in crypto is best understood not as eliminated, but *recomposed.* We no longer rely solely on institutional brands, but on open-source codebases, validator incentives, and the collective alignment of decentralised actors. This creates resilience—but also demands vigilance. Trust becomes something you *audit*, not something you *assume.* You trust the protocol because you can inspect its logic, see its transaction history, review its audits, and watch its governance in real time. But this transparency only helps if you know what to look for. In a decentralised world, *trust is not given—it is earned through understanding.*

This is both empowering and exacting. It shifts responsibility onto the user. The ability to interact with a global financial system without permission is remarkable. But it comes with a cost: you must become literate in the systems you use. Passive trust is replaced by active inquiry. Blind faith is replaced by structural awareness. The days of delegating all responsibility to a financial intermediary are fading. What replaces them is not utopia, but a demanding kind of freedom.

And yet, this is the point. The movement from institutions to protocols is not a rejection of trust—it is a reclaiming of it. Not because everyone becomes an expert overnight, but because the architecture of trust becomes inspectable, contestable, forkable. That's a radical shift. In the legacy system, if your bank fails, your recourse is bureaucratic. In crypto, if a protocol fails or drifts, the community can fork it—clone the codebase, migrate the users, and build something better. The capacity for exit is embedded in the system. This transforms power. It doesn't remove it, but it makes it negotiable.

As we move deeper into a world of programmable trust, the distinction between institutions and protocols will continue to blur. Central banks are exploring digital currencies. Traditional finance is experimenting with tokenised assets. Regulatory frameworks are adapting to the realities of decentralised networks. The hybrid future will be uneven, contested, and complex. But the direction of travel is clear: trust is no longer anchored exclusively in institutions. It is being redefined in code.

The task now is to engage with that code—not blindly, not fanatically, but critically. To understand how it structures incentives, distributes power, and handles failure. To ask not just *what* the protocol does, but *how* it defines trust—and whether that definition serves your values, your goals, and your sense of responsibility.

Because in this new architecture, trust is not a background condition. It is a design choice. And every design has consequences.

What Blockchain Actually Solves (and What It Doesn't)

Blockchain is one of the most misunderstood technologies of the 21st century—not because it is too complex to comprehend, but because it has become too easy to mythologise. Since the launch of Bitcoin in 2009, blockchain has been heralded as a cure-all: a neutral infrastructure to replace corrupt institutions, an engine of financial liberation, a secure database immune to tampering, and more recently, the foundation for a decentralised internet. But despite its technical achievements and social momentum, blockchain is not magic. It is a system of trade-offs. It solves a very specific set of problems elegantly, and a much broader set of problems awkwardly, if at all. The key to using blockchain well is knowing the difference.

At its core, blockchain solves *coordination without central trust.* That's it. It allows multiple parties—who may not know or trust each other—to reach agreement on a shared state of data without needing a central authority to oversee or validate the process. This was not a trivial accomplishment. In traditional systems, databases require administrators. Transactions require banks. Agreements require lawyers or courts. Blockchain replaces these trust brokers with code—cryptographically verifiable, publicly auditable, and enforced by economic incentives. The result is a ledger that no single party controls, yet no party can easily manipulate. This is the essence of what blockchain *does*: it provides *credible neutrality* in environments where mutual distrust is the norm.

Bitcoin was the proof of concept. It demonstrated that you could build a monetary system without a central bank. The blockchain served as an incorruptible ledger of transactions, maintained not by an institution, but by a decentralised network of miners who competed to validate and secure the network through a process known as proof of work. The innovation wasn't just the currency—it was the *governance layer* baked into the protocol. Transactions were final not because a clearinghouse approved them, but because the network reached cryptographic consensus.

This model was extended by Ethereum, which introduced programmable smart contracts. Now, not just payments, but complex logic—escrow, auctions, asset issuance—could be executed on-chain. The blockchain became not just a ledger, but a settlement layer. Projects like MakerDAO, Uniswap, and Aave illustrated that entire financial primitives—lending, trading, collateralisation—could be recreated without traditional intermediaries. These applications showcased the technology's capacity to automate trust itself, provided the conditions were right.

But conditions matter. Blockchain excels in contexts where participants are decentralised, where trust is low or asymmetrical, and where data integrity must be ensured without central oversight. It is particularly well-suited to systems that are adversarial by nature: global finance, cross-border value transfer, permissionless access. It works best when institutional guarantees are either unavailable or untrusted.

However, the more one tries to apply blockchain outside of this trustless paradigm, the more its weaknesses come into focus. For all the talk of universal disruption, blockchain is *not* the optimal tool for most data storage problems. It is expensive, slow, and redundant by design. A decentralised ledger maintained across thousands of nodes is vastly less efficient than a centralised database. Querying a blockchain is harder. Updating it is costly. Data availability and storage limitations constrain the kinds of applications that can run entirely on-chain.

Moreover, blockchain cannot guarantee the truth of what enters it. It can preserve the history of data immutably, but it cannot verify the accuracy of off-chain events without additional infrastructure—usually through oracles. These oracles, which supply external data like asset prices or weather conditions, reintroduce a trust vector. If the oracle is compromised, so is the application. This is not a flaw of blockchain per se, but a reflection of its *limited epistemology*: it knows what's inside the chain. It cannot independently know what's happening in the world.

A parallel misconception is the belief that blockchain automatically ensures fairness or decentralisation. This is not inherent to the technology. Blockchain makes decentralisation *possible*, but not inevitable. It provides tools—open participation, consensus, transparency—but how those tools are configured determines the outcome. Some blockchains are more decentralised than others. Some governance models are dominated by a few insiders. Some tokenomics schemes privilege early entrants or insiders with disproportionate power. Blockchain is *structurally agnostic.* It reflects the intentions of its designers and the incentives of its participants. If those are extractive, the protocol will reflect that, regardless of how decentralised it appears.

This is particularly visible in ecosystems where token distribution is heavily skewed. A DeFi protocol may advertise itself as decentralised, but if 70% of its governance tokens are held by the founding team and venture capital investors, the decision-making is effectively centralised. This creates a gap between the *appearance* of decentralisation and its reality. Blockchain doesn't solve governance. It reframes it in code—but the politics persist. Consensus mechanisms do not eliminate power; they reassign it.

Another persistent myth is that blockchain inherently enhances privacy. In fact, most public blockchains are *radically transparent.* Every transaction, balance, and contract interaction is publicly visible. This is by design—transparency enforces accountability. But it also raises privacy challenges. Surveillance on-chain is trivial for those with the right tools. While privacy-enhancing technologies exist—zero-knowledge proofs, mixers, privacy chains—they are not the default. Many users mistakenly believe that crypto offers anonymity when in fact it offers pseudonymity, which is easily broken.

It is also important to note that blockchain alone does not solve economic inequality, platform dependency, or digital disenfranchisement. These are social and structural problems. Blockchain can support tools that mitigate them—through decentralised finance, open access, and borderless participation—but the presence of a blockchain does not guarantee equitable outcomes. In fact, without intentional design, blockchain systems can reinforce existing inequalities. Early adopters, technically savvy users, and those with capital tend to benefit most. Protocols without thoughtful incentives often reproduce the very dynamics they aim to disrupt.

That said, dismissing blockchain because it does not solve *everything* is as misguided as believing it solves *anything*. It is neither panacea nor snake oil. It is a powerful coordination tool—one that is reshaping how we think about value, governance, identity, and access. The mistake is expecting it to work like magic, rather than understanding it as infrastructure. Infrastructure doesn't solve problems on its own—it enables new solutions, often in ways that aren't obvious at first.

Real-world use cases are starting to reflect this. Cross-border payments using stablecoins provide faster, cheaper alternatives to SWIFT transfers. Decentralised autonomous organisations (DAOs) are experimenting with new forms of collective decision-making, enabling global communities to coordinate funds and action without legal entities. In regions with currency volatility or financial exclusion, crypto wallets offer basic financial services where none previously existed. These are not hypothetical futures. They are happening now, albeit unevenly, and often at the edges of mainstream finance.

What's emerging is a more sober view—one that recognises blockchain's strengths without inflating them. Blockchain is *trust infrastructure*. It allows for verifiable, tamper-resistant records in untrusted environments. It enables programmable institutions—

systems that execute policy automatically, without relying on enforcement by humans. And it offers composability: the ability for multiple protocols to interact and build on each other in ways that centralised platforms struggle to replicate.

But for blockchain to be genuinely transformative, it must be applied where it makes *sense.* The logic of "blockchain everything" has already failed. Projects that tokenise without purpose, decentralise without function, or build chains for problems that don't require chains add noise, not value. The future will not be "on-chain" by default. It will be selectively decentralised—where the benefits of transparency, resilience, and permissionlessness outweigh the costs.

For the thoughtful investor or builder, the challenge is discernment. To look beyond hype cycles and ask hard questions: *Does this system require decentralisation? Who benefits from immutability? What are the trade-offs in latency, scalability, or usability?* Not every application needs a blockchain, just as not every coordination problem needs to be decentralised. The discipline lies in knowing when the properties of a blockchain are uniquely suited to the task at hand—and when they're not.

Grounded thinking is what will separate the next wave of meaningful innovation from the last cycle's speculative excess. And that begins with understanding blockchain not as a vague technological promise, but as a precise tool with specific capabilities. It doesn't solve everything. It doesn't need to. What it solves—if used correctly—is enough to reshape entire categories of trust. And that is more than sufficient.

Code, Consensus, and Human Fallibility

One of the most enduring misconceptions in crypto is the idea that blockchain technology operates in a realm of mathematical perfection, immune to the errors, egos, and inconsistencies of human systems. This belief is seductive—particularly for those seeking clarity in a complex, fragile world. The appeal lies in the idea that if rules are enforced by code, outcomes will be fair, reliable, and apolitical. But this view oversimplifies both the design and reality of decentralised networks. *Blockchains are not autonomous machines.* They are sociotechnical systems: composed of software, but governed by people. The assumption that decentralisation removes human bias or fallibility is not only mistaken—it's dangerous.

Every blockchain, no matter how elegant its protocol, begins with human decisions. Someone writes the code. Someone decides the consensus mechanism. Someone sets the monetary policy, the inflation schedule, the slashing conditions for misbehaviour, the quorum thresholds for governance. These choices are not neutral—they are laden with values, assumptions, and trade-offs. And once deployed, they are interpreted, updated, and contested by communities that are, inevitably, human: passionate, fragmented, and imperfect.

Take the development process itself. The myth of code as objective truth ignores how software is actually built. Developers disagree. Bugs are overlooked. Technical debt accumulates. Features are prioritised or postponed based on subjective criteria. Even open-source communities—often praised for their transparency—can develop political bottlenecks. Contributor hierarchies form. Core developers accrue social capital and influence, shaping the future of the protocol well beyond their formal remit. In theory, decentralised development is open to anyone. In practice, the skills, time, and domain knowledge required to meaningfully contribute form a high barrier to entry. This concentrates power, even in systems designed to diffuse it.

Ethereum is illustrative. Despite being one of the most decentralised networks, Ethereum's roadmap has been heavily influenced by a small group of core contributors. The move from proof of work to proof of stake (Ethereum 2.0) was years in the making and required coordination among developers, validators, application teams, and the broader community. Each stage involved disagreement, risk evaluation, and trade-offs—many of which were philosophical, not purely technical. The eventual transition—successful though it was—did not reflect an automatic upgrade pushed by neutral software. It was the outcome of intensive human deliberation and political negotiation. Code did not drive consensus. Consensus shaped the code.

Consensus itself, in blockchain systems, is often treated as if it were a mechanical function. But consensus is not just an algorithm—it is an agreement among participants to adhere to certain rules. In proof of work systems, that agreement is enforced through energy expenditure. In proof of stake, it is maintained by financial bonding and slashing. But in both cases, consensus is *fragile under pressure*. It depends on honest majority behaviour, on economic incentives holding firm, and on the continued willingness of participants to play by the rules. And when those rules become unclear or contested, human judgement takes over.

Hard forks are the clearest expression of this. When a protocol community splits over a technical or philosophical disagreement, the blockchain itself can bifurcate. This has happened multiple times—most famously with Bitcoin and Bitcoin Cash, and with Ethereum and Ethereum Classic. These forks were not the result of code errors. They were the result of *interpretive disagreement*—conflicts over what the code meant, what values should guide its future, and how to respond to unanticipated crises. These are not questions code can answer. They are questions of governance, ethics, and narrative control.

The DAO hack in 2016 remains one of the most important case studies in this regard. A vulnerability in a smart contract allowed an attacker to drain a significant portion of the Ethereum network's funds. The code had behaved *exactly as written*, but not as intended. The Ethereum community was then faced with a choice: should the blockchain be rolled back to reverse the theft, or should the sanctity of immutability be preserved? The decision to fork the network—

creating Ethereum and Ethereum Classic—was not settled by mathematics. It was settled by debate, votes, moral arguments, and ideological convictions. It was a political act dressed in technical language. And it revealed the soft underbelly of decentralised systems: *behind every immutable contract is a mutable community*.

This is not a flaw—it is a feature. But it requires a recalibration of expectations. Investors and participants need to understand that no blockchain operates in a vacuum. Governance, upgrades, security responses, and even consensus rules evolve through processes that are subject to persuasion, lobbying, and sometimes coercion. Validator cartels can form. Developer groups can go rogue or fragment. Token holders can act out of self-interest, short-term gain, or coordinated manipulation. The belief that a decentralised protocol is somehow above human politics is not just naïve—it's negligent.

Even the incentives encoded in a blockchain's economics—staking rewards, inflation schedules, penalty structures—are ultimately human constructs. They aim to shape behaviour, but they can be gamed. Yield farming in DeFi is a clear example. Protocols that were designed to reward long-term participation often ended up attracting short-term extraction. Users optimised for rewards rather than utility, leading to unsustainable cycles of capital rotation and protocol abandonment. These dynamics are not the result of technical failure. They are the result of human agents responding rationally to poorly structured incentives.

This is why the notion of "pure math" in crypto must be rejected. Blockchain is not like physics. It is not governed by immutable laws of nature. It is governed by assumptions—about rational actors, about economic alignment, about protocol loyalty. These assumptions often hold—until they don't. During times of stress, liquidity evaporates, correlations spike, and users behave unpredictably. Black swans emerge not from the codebase, but from the human response to the unexpected.

This underscores the importance of *institutional literacy* in decentralised systems. Participants must understand not just the technical specifications, but the *social layer* that surrounds the protocol. Who has commit access to the codebase? How are upgrades proposed and ratified? What is the distribution of governance tokens, and how active is participation? Is there a credible dispute resolution process? Are there known fault lines in the community? These questions are not ancillary—they are central. Because when things go wrong, it is the answers to these questions that will determine how, and whether, the system recovers.

It also means that *investing in crypto is not just a technical act—it is a sociopolitical one.* When you allocate capital to a protocol, you are backing not just its architecture, but its community, its norms, and its capacity to adapt. You are placing faith not just in code, but in the people who maintain it. And that requires a level of diligence that goes beyond reading whitepapers. It demands ongoing engagement, scepticism, and the humility to recognise that decentralised systems are not immune to failure—they are simply differently exposed.

Importantly, recognising human fallibility in crypto is not a reason for despair. It is a reason for *maturity*. It calls for a more nuanced understanding of what decentralisation can offer—not a utopia, but a different set of tools for coordinating trust, one that requires just as much political awareness as it does technical skill. The best participants in this space are not those who believe in blockchain as gospel, but those who understand its limits and build systems resilient to its failures.

Trust in crypto is not binary. It is layered—distributed across code, consensus, and community. And each layer has its own failure modes. Code can have bugs. Consensus can be manipulated. Communities can fracture. But taken together, they offer a model of robustness that, while imperfect, is often more transparent and contestable than the black boxes of traditional finance.

To invest well in this landscape, you must stop thinking like a spectator of code and start thinking like a participant in an evolving institution. You are not merely choosing assets. You are aligning with systems—systems built and maintained by people. And people, no matter how brilliant or well-intentioned, make mistakes. If you can see that clearly—not cynically, but constructively—you will be positioned to engage with crypto as it actually is: *a profoundly human experiment in how to share power without losing coherence.* That is not pure math. It is something much harder—and far more important.

The Illusion of Perfect Security

One of the most alluring promises of blockchain technology is that it eliminates the need for trust. "Trustless" systems, so the rhetoric goes, liberate us from the vulnerabilities of human error, corruption, and centralised failure. In theory, if the rules are hard-coded and enforcement is automated, risk is contained. But this framing masks a deeper and more inconvenient truth: *trust has not disappeared—it has migrated.* The decentralised architecture may remove intermediaries, but it does not remove uncertainty. What it does is shift the burden of discernment onto the individual. In place of institutional trust, we now face the more complex challenge of *self-trust*—in our tools, our judgment, and our ability to act securely in a system that is unforgiving by design.

Perfect security is a mirage, and the crypto world—despite its cryptographic foundations—is no exception. Even the most robust protocol, the most meticulously audited smart contract, the most sophisticated multisig wallet cannot insulate users from the consequences of their own lapses. The decentralised ethos is premised on control: you hold your keys, you own your assets, you transact without permission. But with that autonomy comes responsibility. Lose your private key, and your funds are gone. Sign a malicious transaction, and no authority will reverse it. No helpline, no chargeback, no recourse. *You are the failsafe.*

This inversion of responsibility is radical, and it's rarely appreciated at the point of entry. Most users interact with crypto through interfaces designed to resemble traditional apps—simple, sleek, frictionless. But the underlying assumptions are completely different. In a centralised bank, forgetting your password is inconvenient. In crypto, forgetting your seed phrase is fatal. This distinction isn't merely technical—it is *existential.* The system treats your intent as indistinguishable from your actions. The blockchain doesn't care whether you meant to send funds to the wrong address or whether your wallet was compromised. What is broadcast is what is recorded. Finality is a feature—and a liability.

This paradox lies at the heart of decentralised security: *the system does not fail, but people do.* And the system makes no allowances for that failure. It's precisely this rigidity that gives blockchain its power. But it also makes it brittle at the edges—particularly where users, not protocols, are the weakest link. Most hacks in the crypto space are not exploits of the underlying blockchain; they are exploits of human behaviour. Phishing, social engineering, key mismanagement, blind signing, contract spoofing—these are the true attack surfaces. The sophistication of an adversary is rarely in breaking code; it's in manipulating trust.

Case studies abound. In 2022, the Ronin Network—used by the popular game Axie Infinity—suffered a $600 million exploit due to compromised validator nodes. The protocol mechanics worked as intended; the problem was in key management and validator collusion. In 2023, users of the LastPass password manager had their seed phrases compromised because encrypted vaults were exfiltrated and then brute-forced. Again, the vulnerability wasn't the blockchain—it was the handling of credentials. These incidents underline a critical point: *technical soundness does not guarantee operational safety.*

Even hardware wallets, long considered the gold standard for self-custody, are not immune to misuse. Many users, lulled into a false sense of invulnerability, become complacent. They store recovery phrases insecurely, share devices across environments, or fail to verify transaction details on the device itself. And increasingly, attacks are targeting this very complacency—using compromised browser extensions, fake apps, or DNS hijacks to trick users into signing malicious transactions. The signature is valid, the result is catastrophic, and the protocol—true to its logic—executes flawlessly.

This is the crux of the illusion. Blockchain security is not about invulnerability; it's about *integrity within assumptions.* The assumptions are that users behave rationally, secure their keys, verify what they sign, and operate within trusted environments. When those assumptions break, so does the safety. No decentralised system can defend against every misuse scenario. The strength of the system is also its inflexibility. It cannot intervene when the threat is you.

This is why maturity in crypto does not begin with technical knowledge—it begins with psychological clarity. Users must internalise that they are no longer protected by institutional buffers. The margin for error is narrow. And the consequences are absolute. This realisation is often uncomfortable, particularly for those raised in systems where forgiveness is embedded into the infrastructure. But discomfort is not a defect. It's a signal of responsibility. And that responsibility can be transformed into power—*if it is acknowledged and prepared for.*

Preparation, in this context, means adopting habits that extend beyond best practices into behavioural discipline. Use of cold storage is not a checkbox—it's a mindset. It implies a willingness to delay access in favour of resilience. Multisig wallets, time-lock contracts, dead man switches—these are not just tools, they are statements of intent. They encode caution into structure. And caution, when practiced deliberately, is a form of strategic trust: *not trust in technology alone, but in your future self's ability to act wisely under pressure.*

Yet even these defences require human maintenance. Multisig schemes are only secure if signers remain reachable and aligned. Cold wallets only protect if retrieval procedures are tested and up to date. Security routines must evolve with context: new devices, new networks, new threat models. Complacency is entropy. The longer assets are held, the greater the likelihood that something—an upgrade, a lost backup, a forgotten PIN—will decay silently until it matters most. The illusion isn't just that security can be perfect; it's that once configured, it can be static. But in decentralised systems, *security is not a one-time setup. It is a living discipline.*

This reframes the relationship between trust and self-sovereignty. The narrative of decentralisation often frames trust as weakness: a relic of institutional dependency. But this is simplistic. In practice, *trust is reintroduced through contextually intelligent proxies.* You trust your hardware wallet manufacturer to ship uncompromised devices. You trust the developers of your wallet software to maintain and secure the codebase. You trust audit firms, open-source contributors, and governance forums to flag vulnerabilities. Even in trust-minimised systems, *some trust remains.* The difference is that you choose it. You assess it. You revise it.

This is why blind faith in technology is as dangerous as blind faith in institutions. The rhetoric of "trustless" systems can obscure the reality that *every system embeds trade-offs.* Trustlessness is not the absence of trust—it is the modularisation of trust. It lets you reassign it, distribute it, reduce it. But it cannot eliminate it. Believing otherwise leads to overconfidence. Overconfidence leads to loss.

Mature engagement with crypto means accepting this. It means approaching every interaction—every contract, every transaction, every custody decision—with a calibrated scepticism. Not paranoia, but inquiry. What assumptions does this system make about my behaviour? What happens if I disappear? Who can recover access? What data do I rely on? What am I not seeing?

This is not just about safety. It's about sovereignty. True digital sovereignty requires *informed trust.* Not reflexive dependence, but conscious delegation. Not maximalist rigidity, but strategic flexibility. It requires cultivating a posture of awareness—one that integrates technical understanding with behavioural realism. And that realism must account not only for external threats, but for internal ones: fatigue, distraction, convenience, hubris.

Because in a system where you are the final authority, *the most important security protocol is not written in code—it's written in habit.* It is how you think under stress. How you prepare for failure. How you respond to uncertainty. These are the layers of security no blockchain can automate.

Perfect security does not exist. What exists is *appropriate security*: a posture of vigilance calibrated to the context, assets, and capacities of the user. It is the ability to navigate uncertainty with clarity, to adopt friction where needed, and to resist the fantasy that any system—decentralised or not—can substitute for personal discernment.

The future of crypto does not belong to those who believe the systems are flawless. It belongs to those who understand their fragility and still choose to engage—carefully, thoughtfully, and on their own terms. Not because they believe the system will protect them, but because they have learned how to protect themselves.

Chapter 3
Your First Wallet Is a Political Act

Ownership in cryptocurrency carries an odd sort of duality. At first glance, it seems refreshingly simple: download a wallet, tuck away your assets, and step out from under the shadow of banks and brokers. Yet beneath that ease lies a more intricate truth—how you hold your crypto is inseparable from how you hold your agency. Custody is not a matter of software alone; it is a statement of politics and philosophy. It signals what kind of independence you seek, what burdens you are prepared to bear, and how far you are willing to go in accepting responsibility. And like every system that redistributes power, crypto rarely announces these stakes outright. It leaves you to discover them—often only after the damage has been done.

For most of modern finance, the default posture has been custodial. Banks, brokers, insurers—all exist to safeguard assets on your behalf, layering them with contracts, oversight, and state-backed assurances. The structure rests on mediation, on the belief that trust can be outsourced. Crypto upends that architecture. To hold your own keys is to cut away the intermediary. You are not merely withdrawing money; you are withdrawing permission. The language usually frames this in terms of security or control, but the deeper truth is political. To custody your assets yourself is to assert sovereignty over your financial identity, to take on the role of ultimate authority.

That authority is no abstraction. It has the weight of consequence. A private key is not just a cryptographic string—it is the lever through which ownership is enacted. It is your bank, your vault, your passport, your ballot. Lose it, and the system discards you. Share it, and the system obeys another in your place. There is no appeal, no hotline, no tribunal. In a world accustomed to reversible mistakes and institutional safety nets, such finality is alien. In crypto, the ledger itself is judge and record. That austere order demands a level of discipline that glossy wallet apps—with their friendly icons and frictionless flows—often conceal from the novice.

It is worth pausing, then, before moving a single coin, before chasing a yield or signing a transaction. Ask yourself plainly: *Whom do I trust to hold what matters most?* The answer is not purely technical. It is cultural, even personal. It reflects how you weigh risk, how you regard privacy, how much responsibility you believe you can shoulder. For some, the answer is absolute: sovereignty at any cost. For others, the balance of convenience, delegation, or redundancy proves more compelling. There is no universal "right" stance—only an informed one. What proves most dangerous is to drift unthinkingly into a custody model without grasping what it commits you to.

Consider the common distinction between hot and cold wallets. Technically, it refers to connectivity—online versus offline, exposed versus insulated. But beneath that lies a lifestyle declaration. A hot wallet says: *I prize speed, immediacy, access.* A cold wallet says: *I prize permanence, caution, durability.* These are not mere storage options; they are signals of time preference, of financial temperament. Are you trading daily, or building patiently? Do you seek agility, or fortification? Every custody choice encodes a worldview, whether you acknowledge it or not.

Yet the culture of crypto tends to flatten these nuances. Newcomers are nudged toward default settings, told to jot down a seed phrase without ceremony, and often lulled by the notion that security is a chore to revisit later. But custody is not a step in the onboarding funnel—it is the ground beneath it. It deserves to be treated less as an administrative task and more as a rite of passage. Setting up a wallet is not just a technical hurdle; it is a moment of self-recognition, the point at which you assume the obligations of financial adulthood in a system that will not bail you out.

That adulthood is often defined by how you face irreversibility. The internet is littered with cautionary tales: the engineer who tossed out a hard drive containing thousands of Bitcoins; the investor who miswrote a single word of a seed phrase; the wealthy early adopter who locked themselves out with "unbreakable" security. These stories sound like anomalies, but they are structural artefacts of a system that couples freedom with unforgiving logic.

What they reveal, however, is that loss in crypto cuts deeper than financial setback. When you misplace your keys, you lose not only value but also identity and agency. You are reduced to a ghost, present in the system yet stripped of recognition. The lesson here is not despair but respect—for the uncompromising order of the ledger, for the gravity of your choices. Wallet setup, then, ought to be ritual rather than routine. Where are you storing your recovery phrase? Who could gain access to it? What happens if you vanish—or if someone else discovers it first?

Such questions are not idle. They define the perimeter of your autonomy. They shape your investor's psyche, not just your strategy. Those who grasp the stakes of custody act differently. They hesitate before clicking. They rehearse their recovery steps. They prioritise intention over impulse. They understand that convenience today can mean fragility tomorrow.

In the end, custody is culture. It is the practice of clarifying what you protect, why it matters, and how much risk you are willing to make your own. It is not something you configure once and forget. It is a posture—one that can be cultivated, refined, deepened. Custody is the meeting place of liberty and foresight, of ambition and humility. It is where digital self-trust is either confirmed or quietly eroded, decision by decision.

This discussion is not about prescribing a particular wallet or workflow. It is about seeing plainly that your custody choices mirror your convictions about money, power, and governance. They determine not just how you interact with crypto, but how you narrate your role within it. What follows will explore the tangible trade-offs between hot and cold storage, the practicalities of setting up a wallet with awareness, and the psychological burden of key loss as a slow erosion of digital identity. Above all, it will challenge you to treat custody not as clerical housekeeping but as authorship—an intentional shaping of your financial story.

Because in this domain, to hold your own keys is more than a technical function. It is a moral stance. And like all meaningful stances, it requires clarity—not comfort.

Why Custody Is Culture

In the world of crypto, the question of custody is not merely technical—it is ideological. How you store your digital assets reveals more than your understanding of security protocols; it signals your relationship to risk, responsibility, and personal sovereignty. Custody, in this context, is not just about choosing between a hot wallet and a cold wallet. It is an expression of your values. And the decision of whether to entrust your assets to a third-party exchange or to take full control over them is, at its core, a cultural stance.

At the surface level, custody is often framed as a trade-off between convenience and security. But beneath this binary lies a more profound tension—between dependence and independence, between outsourcing risk and owning it entirely. This is where the concept of *custody as culture* becomes critical. Just as the way we manage our money, our homes, or our health reflects deeper psychological orientations, the method by which one handles private keys and wallets speaks volumes about their readiness for digital autonomy.

The idea that decentralised assets could be held in a centralised fashion is, at best, paradoxical. And yet, the vast majority of crypto holders today rely on centralised exchanges or custodial platforms to safeguard their holdings. This is not a purely rational decision—it is a behavioural one. Custodial choices are often shaped by convenience, habit, or fear of technological complexity. But the ramifications of those choices are profound: when you outsource custody, you also outsource control, privacy, and ultimately, accountability.

In traditional finance, most individuals never hold their money in any literal sense. They rely on banks, brokers, and payment providers to facilitate access and security. The infrastructure is built around *delegated trust.* But crypto was architected around a different paradigm—*trust minimisation.* The blockchain itself does not ask you to believe in an institution; it asks you to verify cryptographic proofs. In such a system, custody becomes a form of agency. To hold your own keys is to hold your own fate.

This shift introduces a new psychological landscape, one where empowerment and anxiety coexist. With great control comes great exposure. If you lose your hardware wallet, misplace your seed phrase, or fall for a phishing attack, there is no call centre to reverse the transaction. For some, this feels like liberation. For others, it is a burden too heavy to bear. But either way, it is a conscious reckoning with the idea that sovereignty has a price—and that price is vigilance.

Consider the political implications. In jurisdictions where financial surveillance is routine, the ability to self-custody assets offers a powerful form of resistance. Not resistance in the revolutionary sense, but in the dignified sense of preserving personal privacy. The same technology that allows a teenager in Singapore to buy a fraction of Bitcoin also allows a dissident in Belarus to receive donations without government interference. In both cases, custody becomes a proxy for control over one's economic identity.

Yet the narrative of self-custody is not without its complexities. There is a tendency within crypto discourse to romanticise it—portraying hardware wallets as symbols of rugged individualism. But sovereignty is not just about opting out; it's about what you opt into. Taking custody means accepting the full spectrum of responsibility, including the possibility of self-sabotage. It means confronting your own cognitive and emotional blind spots: your susceptibility to panic, your aversion to learning complex systems, your willingness to skip backups or reuse passwords. These are not technical deficiencies—they are cultural markers.

In this way, custody is an unflinching mirror. It reflects not only your understanding of crypto infrastructure but also your maturity as an economic actor. Many investors approach digital assets with a speculative mindset—buy low, sell high, repeat. But few approach it with the seriousness of stewardship. And yet, the act of custody requires precisely that: a long-term, ethically anchored view of what it means to hold, not just to trade.

One practical example illustrates the difference. A user who holds Bitcoin on a custodial exchange benefits from instant liquidity, sleek interfaces, and customer support. But that same user is also exposed to third-party risk. Exchanges can be hacked, frozen by regulators, or disabled during peak volatility. On the other hand, a user who stores Bitcoin on a cold wallet assumes technical complexity, slower access, and the need for regular maintenance. But they also gain full control—over the asset, the metadata, and the transaction flow. Neither option is inherently right or wrong. What matters is alignment: *Does your method of custody reflect your actual values?*

This question becomes even more pressing as crypto adoption grows and the lines between decentralisation and recentralisation blur. New platforms emerge offering "hybrid custody" solutions—part managed, part user-controlled. Wallets are built with recovery services, social safeguards, and automatic cloud backups. These features reduce friction, but they also shift the cultural balance back toward dependency. The risk is that in making crypto more accessible, we make it less sovereign.

To be clear, not everyone needs—or wants—to be a digital frontiersperson. The goal is not to fetishise self-custody but to understand its philosophical and practical implications. It is entirely legitimate for someone to prioritise ease of use over maximal security, just as it is valid for someone to prefer decentralised finance over traditional banks. What is not legitimate is making that decision unconsciously.

Because when things go wrong—and they often do in crypto—it is the unexamined assumptions that hurt the most. People are surprised when a trusted platform goes under, or when withdrawals are suspended without notice, or when a forgotten passphrase locks them out forever. But these outcomes are not black swans; they are baked into the architecture of a system designed to minimise institutional reliance. The system assumes that you will take ownership of your decisions. If you don't, it will not rescue you.

This introduces a powerful inversion. In traditional finance, the system is designed to protect the user from themselves. In decentralised finance, the system is designed to empower the user—even if that empowerment leads to loss. This is the cultural rift at the heart of crypto custody. It is not just a technical challenge to be solved; it is a civic posture to be adopted. And like any posture, it requires both strength and balance.

So when we ask, *"Where do you keep your crypto?"*, we are also asking, *"What do you believe about freedom, fragility, and the future of finance?"* We are asking whether you trust yourself more than you trust an institution. Whether you are willing to trade convenience for control. Whether you see your role in this ecosystem as a customer, or as a citizen.

These are not small questions. They are the silent architecture beneath every tap, click, and transaction. And they will shape not only how you hold your assets, but how you hold yourself in a decentralised world.

Hot vs Cold: Not Just a Temperature Difference

The decision between using a hot wallet or a cold wallet is often presented as a matter of technical preference, a binary choice in the domain of cybersecurity. But this framing undersells the true weight of the decision. It is not just about software or hardware—it is about identity, behaviour, and how you engage with the digital assets you own. Behind the jargon of 'hot' and 'cold' lies a deeper set of questions: *How often do you need access to your assets? How much control are you willing to assume? And what kind of investor—or digital citizen—are you becoming?*

Let's start with the basics: hot wallets are connected to the internet; cold wallets are not. This simple technical distinction carries profound lifestyle consequences. A hot wallet, whether it's a mobile app like MetaMask or a browser extension linked to a decentralised exchange, offers speed, ease of use, and constant availability. It is designed for daily interactions—swapping tokens, participating in DeFi protocols, sending payments, minting NFTs. It is, in many ways, the functional equivalent of a chequing account: fluid, immediate, and active.

A cold wallet, on the other hand, exists in deliberate isolation. It may take the form of a hardware device like a Ledger or Trezor, or even a piece of paper with a carefully recorded seed phrase, stored in a secure place. It is your digital vault. Not designed for regular interaction, but for long-term preservation. It represents not activity but intent: assets placed in cold storage are not meant to be moved casually. The friction is by design. And that friction is a feature, not a bug.

But to understand what's really at stake, we must look beyond features and into behaviours. Hot wallets encourage immediacy. The barrier to action is low, which makes them ideal for those actively engaged in the markets. But the same immediacy also invites impulsiveness. The investor who checks their wallet five times a day is more susceptible to reactionary decisions—panic selling during a dip, or jumping into the latest altcoin because it's trending on Twitter. In this sense, hot wallets can become psychological accelerants. They reward the same attention loops that social media exploits: short-term thinking, fear of missing out, dopamine hits from price fluctuations.

Cold wallets, conversely, represent delayed gratification. They demand a mindset of stewardship rather than speculation. To use one is to declare: "I do not need this now." And that statement, simple as it is, separates the long-term investor from the opportunist. Cold storage isn't just a method; it's a philosophy. It says that some things are worth preserving with care, beyond the reach of immediate access, and outside the noise of daily volatility. It signals trust in time, not trend.

This is where lifestyle considerations begin to eclipse technical ones. Are you the type of person who wants to actively trade, experiment with decentralised finance, or flip NFTs? Then a hot wallet may be appropriate—though with proper safeguards. Are you holding Bitcoin or Ethereum with the belief that they represent generational assets, long-term stores of value? Then cold storage is not just safer—it is more aligned with your thesis.

But alignment requires honesty. Many people say they are long-term investors, yet keep all their assets in a hot wallet. Or they speak of digital sovereignty, but rely entirely on a custodial exchange to manage their private keys. These inconsistencies are not just operational risks—they are philosophical ones. Because the tools we use shape our habits, and our habits shape our thinking.

The risk profile between hot and cold wallets is not abstract. It is real, measurable, and frequently illustrated by loss. The majority of successful crypto attacks happen via hot wallets—through phishing, malware, browser hijacks, and compromised seed phrases. Attackers know that always-connected systems are the softest targets. Cold wallets, especially those used correctly with offline backups and physical protections, are orders of magnitude harder to breach. The most secure cold wallets are air-gapped—never connected to the internet at all.

But even this security comes with trade-offs. Cold wallets introduce logistical friction. If you want to access your funds, you need the physical device, the passphrase, and often a secondary device for verification. This is not a tool for convenience. It is a tool for commitment. And that commitment needs to be matched with competence—understanding how backups work, where to store your recovery phrase, how to test transactions without exposing your security.

There is also the human factor. People lose hardware wallets. They forget PINs. They write down seed phrases and then accidentally throw them out, mistaking them for scribbled notes. Cold wallets may be technologically secure, but they are not immune to human error. Which means they require not only careful planning but also emotional resilience. If you store assets you cannot afford to lose without adequate safeguards or knowledge, the very security of cold storage becomes a liability.

That is why the hot vs cold question is not about choosing the "best" wallet universally. It is about choosing the wallet that best matches *who you are right now*—not just as an investor, but as a person. Are you diligent, cautious, and self-aware? Cold storage may serve you well. Are you new to crypto, still learning the ropes, unsure about how to recover a wallet if something goes wrong? Then perhaps a trusted custodial platform is a better starting point, at least until your confidence and competence grow.

For many, the optimal solution is a hybrid strategy—using both types of wallets for different purposes. Active funds for trading and engagement remain in a hot wallet, while savings, long-term holds, or high-value assets are secured in cold storage. But even this balanced approach requires intention. The lines between these two domains must be clearly drawn, with thought given to access, inheritance, and emergency planning. Otherwise, what begins as a safety measure becomes an operational tangle.

And this brings us back to the heart of the matter. The decision between hot and cold storage is not just a matter of cybersecurity; it is a matter of self-knowledge. It asks: *What do you value more—access or assurance? Are you prepared to manage risk actively, or do you prefer to isolate it? Is your approach to investing rooted in reaction or reflection?*

Each wallet type makes a claim on your time, your habits, and your psychological bandwidth. A hot wallet whispers, *"Stay ready."* A cold wallet declares, *"Stay disciplined."* Both have their place. But you cannot wield them well unless you understand what they are asking of you.

The real cost of using the wrong wallet is not just financial—it is behavioural. Hot wallet users may become addicted to market noise, always a click away from a decision they regret. Cold wallet users may become complacent, forgetting how to access funds or becoming paralysed by the fear of making a mistake. The right custody setup is not only about how much you hold, but how well your tools reinforce the mindset you want to cultivate.

Ultimately, every wallet is a mirror. Not of the market, but of your temperament. Your tolerance for ambiguity. Your relationship to control. Your ability to delay action until action is truly required. Choosing between hot and cold storage, then, is choosing a rhythm—of trust, of access, of engagement. And the wisest investors are those who choose that rhythm consciously, matching their tools to their time horizon and their temperament alike.

Setting Up Your First Wallet, Intentionally

Setting up a crypto wallet is often treated as a mechanical task: download the app, write down the seed phrase, click "confirm," and move on. But this moment—when you first assume custody over your digital assets—is far more than a routine. It is a threshold, one of the few times in modern life when you take explicit responsibility for your own wealth without the intermediation of an institution. Done carelessly, it's just another app install. Done consciously, it's a shift in sovereignty. This isn't merely a technical setup; it's a declaration of autonomy.

The wallet is not just where your crypto lives. It's where your intent lives. It holds your money, yes, but also your memory, your attention, and, most crucially, your risk. When you create a wallet, you're not just gaining access—you're becoming accountable. There is no customer service line to reset your password, no third party to retrieve your funds. This finality is both frightening and freeing, depending on how prepared you are to handle it.

Approaching this setup with awareness means recognising that your first wallet experience will shape your behaviours, assumptions, and comfort levels for years to come. The habits you build now—how you store keys, how you verify addresses, how you react to error—will either compound into confidence or spiral into fragility. So rather than rushing through the process, treat it as a moment worth slowing down for. Like lighting a fire for the first time, it demands attention, patience, and respect.

Begin by deciding *what role this wallet will play* in your financial life. Will it be a hot wallet for small, frequent transactions? A vault for long-term holdings? A test wallet for learning and experimentation? Clarity on use-case is foundational—because the trade-offs between accessibility and security are real, and your configuration should reflect your actual behaviour, not your aspirational self-image.

Next, consider the environment in which you'll create the wallet. Are you doing it on a public Wi-Fi network, with browser extensions active and ten tabs open? Or have you taken the time to disable distractions, use a dedicated device, and scan for malware? Many compromises don't come from high-tech exploits, but from low-awareness environments. *Security is often less about sophistication and more about intentionality.*

When you generate your seed phrase—the master key to your digital assets—you are holding something with more power than a bank card, yet with none of the protections. Write it down, yes, but more importantly: decide where it belongs in your life. Will you store it in a safe, split it into parts and store across locations, use a metal backup plate to resist fire or water damage? Whatever the method, ensure that it reflects your actual discipline, not just theoretical best practice. A strategy you won't follow is worse than none at all.

And then, there is the question few guides address: *Who else should know about your wallet?* For many, setting up a wallet is a solitary act. But this isolation creates a vulnerability: what happens if something happens to you? Who inherits access? This isn't just estate planning; it's moral planning. Do you trust a family member, a lawyer, or a multisig arrangement? Setting up your first wallet is the first time many users are confronted with the broader implications of financial self-custody—including the reality that sovereignty without succession is fragile.

Equally important is the ritual of verification. Before sending any funds, test the setup. Send a small amount. Receive it. Withdraw it. Understand the interface. Many losses occur not because of malicious hacks, but because people didn't test their setup before transferring significant value. The confidence that comes from performing small, intentional transactions is vastly underrated—and vastly more important than rushing to stake, swap, or save on fees.

Too often, users treat wallets like tools they can swap at will. But in reality, they are more like homes. Where you store your assets shapes how you interact with them. A wallet with a sleek interface might encourage more frequent activity, while a hardware wallet, by introducing friction, nudges you toward longer-term thinking. These behavioural nudges are subtle but powerful. Choosing your wallet, then, is not just about selecting features—it's about choosing your future tendencies.

There is also the matter of digital hygiene. If your wallet is software-based, consider the device it lives on. Is your phone updated? Do you use biometric authentication or a strong passcode? Do you click links impulsively? Wallet security is deeply tied to *device hygiene and user habits*. A careless tap on a phishing link can drain a wallet in seconds. Setting up your first wallet should come with the same care you'd apply to setting up an alarm system—not because you expect danger at every turn, but because *you understand what's at stake.*

And yet, caution alone is not enough. Confidence matters too. The point of setting up your wallet intentionally is not to become paranoid—it's to become grounded. To understand what you're doing, why it matters, and how to revisit it over time. Your wallet setup isn't a one-off task; it's a system that should evolve with you. Maybe you start with a single seed phrase written on paper. Over time, you move to multisig. Eventually, you teach someone else how to manage it. *This arc reflects not just growing assets, but growing maturity.*

All of this circles back to a simple but profound idea: *your wallet reflects your philosophy*. If you value independence, your setup should honour that with cold storage and recovery planning. If you prioritise ease of use, acknowledge the risks and adapt with mitigations—smaller balances, stricter device hygiene, or staged withdrawal thresholds. There is no universally perfect setup. There is only the setup that reflects your actual values, routines, and limitations.

Some users will skim this process and regret it later. But for those willing to pause and do it consciously, the rewards are outsized—not just in terms of security, but in personal clarity. Setting up your wallet is the moment crypto becomes real. The moment you move from concept to contact. From watching to participating. It's not just a task; it's a transition.

And like all meaningful transitions, it is best approached not with haste, but with presence. Ask yourself: *Do I understand what I am securing? Do I understand how this tool works? Do I understand the responsibility I'm accepting?* If the answer to any of these is "no," then that is not failure. That is the point at which you begin—not with bravado, but with curiosity, patience, and care.

Done this way, setting up a wallet becomes more than a means to an end. It becomes an expression of who you are in the digital world. Not just a user, but a steward. Not just a speculator, but a participant in a broader, decentralised experiment in trust, freedom, and agency. And that, in itself, is worth doing with your full attention.

Losing Keys, Losing Identity

When people think of losing money, they tend to imagine a scam, a market crash, or a miscalculated trade. In crypto, however, some of the most catastrophic losses occur not from theft or volatility—but from simple forgetfulness. A misplaced notebook, a wiped hard drive, an old phone tossed out without backup. These seemingly trivial lapses have rendered millions, even billions, of pounds' worth of digital assets permanently inaccessible. In decentralised finance, there is no customer support line, no "forgot password" option. The system is designed to eliminate intermediaries, but that design comes with a stark truth: *if you lose your keys, you lose everything*. And not just your funds—but your standing, your confidence, your sense of digital self.

James Howells, a British IT worker, became globally known for accidentally throwing away a hard drive in 2013 containing the private keys to 8,000 Bitcoins—now worth hundreds of millions. He had mined them back when Bitcoin was a curiosity, not a currency. The hard drive ended up in a landfill in Newport, and years later, he was still campaigning to excavate it, battling local councils for permission. His story is often told with a tinge of dark comedy, but what it represents is deeply sobering: that a person can have access to vast wealth *in theory*, yet none of it in practice—all because of one discarded device and a forgotten ritual of backup.

This is not just a technical issue. It's a philosophical one. Crypto custody represents a unique form of ownership—one where possession is not nine-tenths of the law, but all of it. The private key *is* the asset. Lose the key, and what remains on the blockchain is merely an unspendable ghost of value. There's no judge who can override the protocol, no administrator who can reset your credentials. This finality—so unlike the reversibility of traditional finance—exposes how fragile our relationship with responsibility truly is.

For many, this fragility is only understood after the fact. Take the example of Stefan Thomas, a programmer who received 7,002 Bitcoins for making an educational video on cryptocurrency. He stored the keys on an encrypted IronKey USB drive and forgot the password. After ten failed attempts, the device locks permanently. With only two tries left, Thomas lives in a limbo of digital purgatory—so close, yet permanently out of reach. He spoke openly about the emotional toll: the obsessive nights, the mental spiral, the paralysis of regret. This isn't just financial loss—it's existential loss. Because what he lost was not just money, but the illusion of control.

These stories are not outliers. Chainalysis, a blockchain analytics firm, estimates that roughly 20% of all Bitcoins—potentially worth over $100 billion—are "lost" due to forgotten keys or discarded wallets. And those are just the documented cases. What they reveal is a deeper truth: that most people are psychologically unprepared for absolute sovereignty. We have grown used to the idea that there's always someone we can call, some system we can appeal to, some recovery process we can initiate. Crypto erases that safety net—and in doing so, *tests our maturity.*

That test begins with custody. Most new users treat wallet setup as a checklist item—something to be rushed through in the excitement of buying tokens or joining an airdrop. Few pause to ask: *where am I storing my key? What happens if I'm hit by a car? Who else could access this? Am I backing up out of discipline or out of fear?* These questions are rarely technical. They are psychological. *They force us to confront the limits of our attention, our memory, our rituals, and our self-respect.*

There's a reason ancient cultures developed rituals around money and inheritance. Wealth has always demanded care. Yet in the digital age, that care is often outsourced. Password managers, biometrics, cloud backups—we've externalised responsibility to the point where we've forgotten how to carry it ourselves. Crypto reverses that trend. It says: the vault is not in a bank; it is in your habits. And if your habits are sloppy, no amount of technical security will protect you.

Careless custody is not just a technical mistake—it's an ethical one. It signals that you value access over stewardship, that you want the benefits of sovereignty without the burden. But ownership without responsibility is hollow. To hold crypto and fail to secure it is like owning a house and leaving the doors open—not out of courage, but out of negligence. It disrespects not only your own effort, but the trust embedded in the decentralised ethos itself.

There's also a quiet social cost to key loss. People rarely speak of the shame that accompanies it—the internal narrative of self-blame, the external fear of ridicule. When money disappears due to hacks or scams, the victim often finds sympathy. But when it vanishes due to carelessness, the silence is deafening. Few want to admit they misplaced a phrase that could have changed their life. And so, these incidents become private tragedies—ones that erode confidence, not just in the technology, but in oneself.

This is why preventative wisdom is paramount. Key security should be treated like a sacred ritual. Not out of paranoia, but out of respect—for your future self, for your time, for the integrity of the system. Write it down, store it well, test your backups, rotate your access occasionally. Use multisig if the amounts are substantial. Educate someone you trust. And above all, *don't let convenience dictate your custody*. Because the easiest way today may be the most painful tomorrow.

There are, of course, innovations aimed at solving this fragility—social recovery wallets, biometric safeguards, smart contract vaults. These are promising, but none remove the need for awareness. They may make custody more forgiving, but they cannot make it wise. That is still a human function. And wisdom is not built through convenience—it is built through *conscious design of habit.*

What's at stake here is more than money. It's a kind of digital dignity. To lose your keys is to lose your agency. To protect them is to affirm your readiness. This is why key management is not a boring security footnote, but a profound ethical act. It is where sovereignty begins—or where it silently dies.

So before you laugh at the man digging through a landfill, or shrug off the story of the locked USB, ask yourself: *Could that be me? Have I earned the right to hold my own assets?* If the answer is uncertain, don't despair. Let that uncertainty be a signal—not of failure, but of a readiness to grow.

Crypto does not forgive, but it teaches. And one of its first, hardest, and most lasting lessons is this: *you are your own vault.* And whether that vault is respected or neglected is up to you.

Chapter 4
Exchanges Are Not Neutral

Most first-time investors picture a cryptocurrency exchange as something neutral and blandly functional—like an online broker or a banking portal. You sign up, wire in some fiat, and start buying coins. But the reality runs deeper. Beneath that tidy interface sits an entire architecture—technical, cultural, political—that shapes how you participate. Exchanges are not anonymous pipes shuttling liquidity. They are entities with their own agendas, temperaments, and incentives. To choose one is not just to pick a service; it is to align yourself, however subtly, with its values. And those values, over time, shape yours.

At surface level, centralised exchanges—Coinbase, Binance, Kraken, and the like—offer similar packages: fiat onramps, trading pairs, mobile apps, staking options, customer support. Yet scratch at the veneer and contrasts emerge. Coinbase, publicly traded in the United States, cultivates an image of regulatory faithfulness: compliance-heavy, cautious, polished. Binance, dominant in volume, carries the baggage of opaque structures, jurisdictional skirmishes, and uneasy regulatory entanglements. Kraken, meanwhile, embraces libertarian tones, preferring resilience and security over glossy onboarding. These are not cosmetic distinctions. They determine how user data is stored, how swiftly assets can be frozen, which tokens are listed, how regulators are confronted—or appeased. To sign up is to enter into an ideological relationship, whether you acknowledge it or not.

That relationship begins the moment you onboard. For the uninitiated, the process feels almost ceremonial: the KYC prompts, ID scans, selfies uploaded to faceless systems, the long pauses of verification. It is often the first time a newcomer realises that crypto, paradoxically, may require more personal exposure than their bank ever did. But onboarding need not overwhelm. Approached calmly, with intention, it can be clarifying. Where am I willing to place my identity? What legal protections—or vulnerabilities—come with this jurisdiction? How easily can I exit later? Few ask such questions in haste, but the thoughtful investor makes time.

Exchanges, however, are not neutral hosts. They thrive on volume and volatility, and so their interfaces are engineered to accelerate you. Airdrops, referral bonuses, trading badges, flashing tickers—all designed to push you forward. Speed feels like efficiency, but in finance it is often the enemy of discernment. The quicker you click, the less you pause; the less you pause, the more likely you move in service of the platform's revenue rather than your own strategy. Convenience has a cost, though it rarely shows up on the fee schedule. The first cost is attention itself—its erosion, its capture.

The second cost lies in custody. When you deposit crypto into a centralised exchange, it does not sit in a vault with your name on it. It flows into pooled accounts under the platform's control. What you see on your dashboard is a claim on that pool, not a private key in your possession. There are benefits—faster withdrawals, operational safeguards, institutional-grade defences—but also a fragility. Hacks, insolvency, mismanagement: if the exchange falters, so do you. Mt. Gox in 2014 and FTX in 2022 remain cautionary monuments. In both, users discovered that trust in the platform was less shield, more liability.

Even withdrawals—the act of reclaiming what is yours—are not always straightforward. Some platforms impose steep fees, delays, or thresholds. Others throttle exits when markets panic. The friction is rarely advertised; it emerges when you most need freedom. Retained liquidity is a strategic asset for an exchange, and if that means slowing your exit, so be it. The wise investor writes their exit plan before committing funds. If you cannot leave on your terms, you never truly entered.

Politics, though less visible, are everywhere in exchanges. Listings, delistings, country bans, token airdrops—none of these are neutral. They reflect legal pressures, business deals, strategic manoeuvres. When Coinbase delists under regulatory shadow, or Binance services sanctioned regions via elaborate shells, those are not technical events but political stances. Users are drawn into these stances whether they wish it or not. Neutrality, in this domain, is myth.

Visibility is another trade-off. On a centralised exchange, you are legible: your trades, deposits, withdrawals, IP, even browsing habits are captured, and often shared. Many come to crypto seeking pseudonymity, only to find themselves more transparent than in traditional finance. Decentralised protocols such as Uniswap or Thorchain allow pseudonymous interaction; CEXs demand names, documents, histories. Some investors will accept this, others will not—but what matters is entering with awareness, not discovering too late.

None of this is to say exchanges are villains. They supply vital liquidity, education, infrastructure. But to engage with them wisely requires seeing them for what they are: not utilities, but curated environments with built-in biases. A seasoned investor neither demonises nor sanctifies them. The point is not abstention, but clarity—knowing the terms of the relationship, using the platform with intent rather than being used by it.

This chapter is designed to sharpen that clarity. It will guide you through reading platforms not by their glossy claims but by their incentives. It will suggest how to approach verification with composure, how to measure the hidden costs of interface convenience, how to think about withdrawal before deposit. Exchanges are not mere gateways. They are cultural spaces. Spaces that reflect and, over time, reshape you—not just as an investor but as a participant in a new financial order.

Once you absorb that exchanges are never neutral, they cease to appear inevitable. They become what they always were: choices. And real choice begins not with hype or urgency, but with the kind of knowledge that resists both—the quieter kind, anchored in awareness rather than noise.

The Personality of Platforms

When most people think about choosing a cryptocurrency exchange, they imagine a neutral service: a functional marketplace where orders are matched, balances are displayed, and transactions are processed. But this assumption glosses over one of the most critical—and underexamined—aspects of crypto investing: *platforms are not neutral.* They are not simply infrastructure; they are institutions, each embedded with a distinct culture, ideology, and incentive structure. They are not interchangeable storefronts, but philosophical propositions wearing the clothing of convenience. And choosing where to trade, store, and interact is not just a technical decision—it's a declaration of alignment.

To understand an exchange is to examine what it optimises for, whom it serves, and how it interprets the balance between control and freedom. Coinbase, Binance, and Kraken—the three most globally recognised platforms—illustrate this vividly. On paper, they offer similar services: spot trading, staking, fiat gateways, and token listings. But their design language, compliance posture, governance decisions, and user relationships diverge sharply. These differences matter—not just in times of crisis, but in the everyday habits they encourage, the risks they conceal, and the assumptions they make about the user's role in the ecosystem.

Coinbase positions itself as the polished ambassador of crypto to the traditional financial world. Based in the United States and publicly listed on Nasdaq, it has made regulatory clarity a central part of its brand. Its clean user interface, bank-level KYC protocols, and strategic partnerships with Wall Street institutions all communicate one thing: safety through assimilation. If Coinbase has a personality, it's institutional conservatism wrapped in tech optimism. This appeals to users who seek legitimacy, compliance, and ease of access. But it also means that Coinbase is highly sensitive to regulatory whims, conservative in token listings, and willing to geo-fence or delist assets to maintain legal standing. For investors who value sovereignty or privacy above regulatory alignment, this ethos may feel restrictive rather than reassuring.

Binance, by contrast, is the digital pirate ship of global crypto markets—agile, aggressive, and unrepentantly opportunistic. With no clear headquarters, a sprawling network of subsidiaries, and a founder who's as much myth as executive, Binance embodies a culture of scale over sentiment. Its innovation velocity is unmatched—new tokens, features, and yield products appear at breakneck speed. But so too do legal disputes, opacity in corporate structure, and abrupt service changes. For investors who value access to everything and can tolerate risk, Binance is intoxicating.

Yet this comes at the price of predictability, transparency, and regulatory goodwill. It is not a platform designed to protect the cautious. It is a platform that assumes you know what you're doing—and if you don't, the market will correct you.

Kraken takes a different path. Founded in the aftermath of Mt. Gox's collapse, Kraken wears its security credentials like a badge of honour. With a deep focus on operational integrity, cold storage, and user education, it appeals to those who value long-term resilience over user experience flash. Kraken's tone is almost academic, often publishing detailed regulatory commentary and taking principled stances on issues like user privacy and asset listings. It's not designed to maximise trading volume. It's designed to preserve trust. Kraken's ethos is that of a stubborn idealist: slower, perhaps, but more durable. Investors who appreciate integrity over immediacy tend to find a philosophical home here.

These profiles are not incidental. They are the product of design choices, executive philosophies, market positioning, and cultural values. And those values bleed into how the platforms function under stress. During the FTX collapse, for example, Kraken's CEO publicly warned about solvency risks while maintaining open channels for withdrawals. Binance, initially hailed as a white knight for the distressed firm, quickly distanced itself, and within days, FTX imploded. Coinbase, meanwhile, ran full-page ads in major newspapers warning of the dangers of unregulated players, positioning itself as the adult in the room. Each response reflected not just crisis management, but worldview. *Crisis reveals character—and in crypto, platforms have character.*

Even in normal times, platforms influence behaviour through subtle nudges. Coinbase's retail app simplifies buying into a few clicks, hiding order book complexity and nudging users toward recurring purchases. Binance offers margin trading, futures, and leveraged tokens directly alongside spot markets, often to retail users who may not fully grasp the risks. Kraken includes detailed market stats and order book depth, encouraging more thoughtful engagement with price mechanics. These interface choices are not neutral. They condition the user. Over time, they shape what kind of investor you become. *If a platform rewards speed, you will chase speed. If it rewards thoughtfulness, you will lean into diligence.*

Beyond interface, there's also the question of what tokens platforms choose to list. This is often mistaken as a question of supply and demand. But listings are political. They signal what kind of innovation a platform supports, what jurisdictions it cares about, and what level of due diligence it considers sufficient. Coinbase has historically taken a conservative path—sometimes lagging months behind other exchanges in listing popular assets. Binance, meanwhile, has faced criticism for listing low-liquidity tokens with questionable fundamentals, only to remove them after they crash. Kraken often sits somewhere in the middle, vetting assets more carefully but with a wider tolerance for decentralised finance experiments. A platform's listing policy is not just about inventory—it's about trust, responsibility, and signal fidelity.

There is also the invisible layer of algorithmic preference. Not all trades are treated equally. Exchanges operate with internal routing systems, liquidity partnerships, and in some cases, proprietary trading desks. These may affect execution prices, slippage, and latency. Retail users rarely see this. But for professionals or observant traders, discrepancies between quoted price and filled price can become meaningful. Platforms that are transparent about these mechanics tend to inspire more long-term trust. Those that obscure them often see higher churn. *The less you understand how an exchange works under the hood, the more you are betting on faith.*

Trust, of course, is the real currency of platforms. And trust is never static—it is earned, lost, or reinforced with every interaction. A delayed withdrawal, an uncommunicated maintenance window, or a sudden policy change can rupture user confidence overnight. Conversely, clear communication, swift response to incidents, and principled transparency can create loyalty that no referral bonus ever could. Users remember how platforms made them feel during moments of uncertainty. And those feelings become the basis for continued use—or decisive exit.

Perhaps the most neglected dimension of platform personality is data ethics. Exchanges collect vast amounts of behavioural, transactional, and identity data. How they store, monetise, and protect that data is largely invisible to users. But it is a dimension of personality that will grow more consequential as governments increase surveillance, and as exchanges grow more entwined with traditional finance. A platform that views your data as an asset to monetise will behave differently from one that views it as a responsibility to protect. *Convenience often masks compromise. And compromise, once normalised, is difficult to reverse.*

Ultimately, the choice of exchange is not just about functionality or liquidity—it's about alignment. Do you want institutional protection or experimental freedom? Do you prefer user simplicity or granular control? Do you value compliance or autonomy? These are not abstract values. They translate into which platform you use, how you interact with it, and what kinds of habits it reinforces. Investors who treat exchanges as neutral tools are flying blind. Investors who understand that platforms have personalities can navigate with intent.

Because in crypto—as in politics, media, or community—the platform *is* the message. And if you don't understand the message your platform is broadcasting, you may be subscribing to a value system you never consciously chose.

Onboarding Without Overwhelm

Most investors remember their first crypto experience not as a thrilling technological awakening but as an intimidating chore. A cluttered interface. Confusing jargon. Endless pop-ups and authentication emails. Screens asking for selfies with passports. Warnings about irreversible transfers. Terms of service longer than tax codes. This is the quiet truth behind crypto's public face: for all its revolutionary promise, the first step into the ecosystem often feels like a test of patience, not empowerment. And for many, that first impression colours everything that follows. *How we begin shapes how we behave.* In crypto, as in most complex systems, clarity is a competitive advantage—and onboarding is where clarity must start.

The word *onboarding* is deceptively clinical. In crypto, it refers not only to creating an account on an exchange or setting up a wallet, but also to verifying your identity, securing your credentials, linking payment methods, and executing your first transaction. These steps form a bridge between traditional finance and digital assets, and how that bridge is built—whether hastily or deliberately—has long-term implications. Done carelessly, it breeds confusion, anxiety, and poor habits. Done intentionally, it becomes the foundation of financial confidence. Yet most guides reduce onboarding to a checklist: Sign up. Upload ID. Connect bank. Buy Bitcoin. That sequence may suffice mechanically, but it misses the deeper opportunity: *to cultivate intentionality in a world optimised for urgency.*

FOMO—fear of missing out—is not just an emotional impulse; it is an interface strategy. Platforms are designed to convert attention into action. They flash green percentages, push limited-time offers, and prompt "one-click" buys, often before a user fully understands what they are purchasing or why. For those new to crypto, this barrage of stimuli creates a sense of performance anxiety—everyone else seems to know what they're doing, and you're trying to catch up. The irony is that this pressure rarely serves the user. It serves the platform. *Urgency drives volume. Volume drives profit.* But investing is not an emergency. The healthiest portfolios are not built in moments of frenzy. They are assembled with clarity, over time, and with restraint.

To avoid overwhelm, the first principle is this: **simplicity is not the absence of information; it is the presence of discernment**. Simplicity means filtering signal from noise, pausing before clicking, and asking yourself a few foundational questions: What am I trying to achieve? What am I comfortable risking? What do I need to understand *before* I transact? These questions are not luxuries—they are critical thinking tools that inoculate against reactive behaviour. They help you recognise when a platform is guiding you thoughtfully versus manipulating your attention.

Let's consider the typical KYC (Know Your Customer) process—a now-standard compliance step where users upload government ID and verify their identity. Technically, this is a legal safeguard to prevent money laundering. But philosophically, it's also a moment of inversion: you are declaring who you are to enter a system built on pseudonymity. This trade-off—privacy for access—should not be glossed over. Some users may be comfortable with it. Others may prefer decentralised alternatives that don't require KYC. What matters is not the choice itself, but that the choice is *conscious*. The worst outcome is sleepwalking into centralised dependence while believing you've joined a decentralised revolution.

Verification is often followed by linking a payment method. Here too, nuance is key. Credit cards offer speed but often come with steep fees. Bank transfers are cheaper but slower. Some exchanges offer third-party integrations like Apple Pay or PayPal, each with their own terms. It's tempting to choose the fastest path, especially when the market appears to be moving. But onboarding is not a race. Rushing through these steps may cost you more—financially and cognitively—than taking a few hours to research each option. *Slowness in onboarding is not hesitation. It is literacy in progress.*

Interface design also plays a pivotal role. Some platforms, like Coinbase, prioritise user-friendliness, hiding complexity beneath intuitive menus. Others, like Kraken or Gemini, surface more technical features and market data from the outset. There is no universal best interface—there is only what suits your current level of knowledge. A good strategy is to start with the most basic mode and gradually unlock complexity as your confidence grows. Many platforms now offer "basic" and "advanced" views. Resist the urge to prove sophistication by jumping into charts and limit orders. *Complexity is seductive, but clarity is productive.*

Beyond design, language matters. Terms like "staking," "gas fees," "network congestion," and "wallet address" are thrown around with casual confidence, but they often mask conceptual complexity. Rather than pretending to understand, pause and research. Use this onboarding period to build vocabulary with rigour. A platform that offers educational prompts, hover-over definitions, or guided walkthroughs is respecting your time and intelligence. A platform that overwhelms you with acronyms and fine print is not. *Intellectual humility is an onboarding superpower.*

One useful mental model is to treat onboarding as a rite of passage, not a transaction. Rites of passage are structured to provoke awareness, discipline, and transformation. They take time. They are not "click-through" experiences. They ask something of you. In crypto, this might mean taking a deliberate afternoon to create strong passwords, enable 2FA (two-factor authentication), back up your recovery phrases, and document your credentials in a secure, offline location. These acts may feel tedious. But they are acts of sovereignty. They signal that you are not merely using crypto—you are *inhabiting* it.

The most resilient investors are not those who bought at the bottom or timed every exit perfectly. They are those who established strong foundations. Foundations begin with onboarding. A password manager. A unique email address. A dedicated device. A habit of reading transaction confirmations twice. These are not paranoid behaviours. They are prudent ones. In a landscape rife with phishing, social engineering, and SIM-swap attacks, every layer of preparation is a defence of agency. *Security is not a setting. It is a mindset nurtured from the start.*

Consider also the emotional dimension. Onboarding can trigger doubt: "Am I doing this right?" "What if I make a mistake?" "Is it too late to get in?" These feelings are not weaknesses. They are signals of engagement. Rather than suppress them, name them. Journal your thoughts. Talk to a friend. Seek out forums or communities that prioritise education over hype. The act of naming your fears converts them from shadows into shapes. And shapes can be understood, managed, and gradually replaced with confidence.

Simplicity becomes a superpower precisely because the crypto ecosystem is so noisy. In a sea of tokens, trading pairs, and update notifications, the ability to focus—to proceed step by step, to ignore irrelevant prompts, to delay non-essential actions—is rare. It's also powerful. Investors who master onboarding with minimal drama often go on to develop cleaner mental models, better record-keeping habits, and a healthier relationship with volatility. They don't chase coins or obsess over price feeds. They trust their setup, because they built it intentionally.

This subchapter is not about which platform to use or which coin to buy first. It is about how to *enter* well. With patience. With preparation. And with the understanding that the path to crypto literacy begins not with a trade, but with a temperament. A temperament that resists distraction, honours detail, and moves with intention—not because there's a rush, but because there's a responsibility.

Your first login is not just the start of your portfolio. It is the start of your philosophy. And how you onboard—whether chaotically or consciously—will echo through every trade, every wallet, and every decision that follows. Simplicity isn't the absence of tools. It is mastery over them.

The Hidden Costs of Convenience

The most dangerous decisions in crypto often appear harmless. No alarms sound when you create an account on a centralised exchange. No warning label blinks when you leave your assets in its custody. It all feels frictionless—smooth, efficient, user-friendly. And that is precisely the problem. Convenience does not signal safety. It signals trade-offs, and in crypto, those trade-offs are rarely declared upfront. *What you gain in speed, you often lose in sovereignty. What you offload in responsibility, you forfeit in control.* Understanding the hidden costs of convenience is not just about protecting your portfolio—it's about defining the kind of relationship you want with your money, your data, and your future autonomy.

Centralised exchanges have played an essential role in crypto adoption. Platforms like Binance, Coinbase, and Kraken lowered the barrier to entry, allowing millions to buy, sell, and store crypto without technical know-how. They brought liquidity, regulatory compliance, and customer support—features that early decentralised platforms lacked. But in solving those problems, they reintroduced an older one: *intermediated trust.* Users may believe they "own" their crypto, but in reality, what they own is an IOU—a database entry governed by terms they likely didn't read, on infrastructure they don't control.

The convenience of custody is the most overlooked hazard. When you leave assets on an exchange, you are not holding them; the exchange is. You do not possess the private keys. You cannot independently verify your balance. You are relying on the platform's infrastructure, security protocols, and risk management practices. That reliance may feel innocuous—until it isn't. When FTX collapsed in 2022, billions in customer funds evaporated overnight. No warning. No recourse. People logged in one day to check their balances and found only silence. What many thought was "their crypto" had never truly belonged to them. *Custody, in crypto, is not a feature. It is a responsibility. And outsourcing it has consequences.*

To be clear, not all centralised exchanges are reckless. Some maintain robust security standards, transparent audits, and strong legal frameworks. But even the best-run platforms are vulnerable to the structural risks of centralisation: single points of failure, internal malfeasance, regulatory freezes, and cyber-attacks. When one platform controls millions of wallets, it becomes a honeypot for attackers and a lever for regulators. That leverage may be used for consumer protection—or it may be used to block withdrawals, freeze assets, or comply with extraterritorial laws. *When you store crypto on a centralised exchange, your financial freedom becomes conditional.*

This is not a theoretical concern. In 2023, Canadian regulators mandated that exchanges block transactions to privacy-related protocols. Users who left their funds on those exchanges had no choice but to comply. In the UK, similar proposals have emerged to restrict access to self-custody wallets under certain AML frameworks. These are not necessarily malicious acts. But they reveal the deeper tension: *convenience centralises power.* When users flock to easy platforms, they concentrate control—technical, financial, and political—into the hands of a few corporate entities. Over time, this reshapes the architecture of crypto itself. *The infrastructure reflects the incentives of its dominant custodians.*

Speed is another form of seduction. Centralised exchanges settle trades instantly. Funds are available immediately. You can swap assets, set limit orders, and track charts in real-time. But this speed comes at a hidden cost: abstraction. You are not interacting with a blockchain. You are interacting with a replica of it, optimised for usability, not transparency. You may not notice the trade-off—until it matters. When withdrawals are paused during market crashes, or when on-chain fees spike and exchanges impose limits, users discover the boundary between simulation and reality. *Speed without sovereignty is a short-term gain with long-term fragility.*

Privacy is also quietly sacrificed. Exchanges require KYC—government-issued IDs, selfies, utility bills. These data points are stored on servers, often indefinitely, subject to hacks or subpoenas. Even if the platform is secure, the user may not be. Reused passwords. Unencrypted backups. Weak 2FA protocols. Each convenience introduces an attack surface, and unlike decentralised systems, centralised exchanges cannot guarantee user anonymity. Your trades, balances, and behaviours can be analysed, correlated, and sold. *The price of convenience is not just paid in fees. It is paid in identity.*

Some argue that these compromises are necessary. That most users prefer convenience. That friction deters adoption. And in some respects, this is true. Not everyone wants to manage seed phrases or run a full node. But *this truth should not be confused with virtue.* Popularity does not equal progress. The early internet thrived on open protocols; then platforms centralised those protocols for convenience. Today, social media networks own your content, cloud services own your data, and financial institutions own your transaction history. Crypto was supposed to reverse this drift. *When exchanges become the new banks, the revolution starts to resemble the regime it sought to replace.*

To be clear, this is not a call to abandon centralised exchanges. They serve real purposes: liquidity, fiat onramps, ease of use. But using them should be a *tactical choice*, not a default habit. The mature investor treats them like train stations, not destinations—places to enter and exit the crypto ecosystem, not places to store long-term wealth. This mindset requires a shift: from passive user to active custodian. From speed-seeker to resilience builder. From customer to participant.

Resilience is perhaps the most undervalued trait in crypto. It is not just about technical robustness—it is about mental discipline. Self-custody is harder. Cold storage is inconvenient. Multi-signature wallets are complex. But each layer of inconvenience is a layer of independence. *The more friction you embrace, the more antifragile your setup becomes*. You learn to test backups. You monitor withdrawal limits. You ask: What happens if this platform disappears? This is not paranoia. It is preparedness.

Convenience, by contrast, dulls these questions. It teaches you to trust the interface, not understand it. To follow prompts, not probe principles. To click "Buy" without reading the fine print. Over time, this breeds a shallow relationship with your assets—one that is easily disrupted by outages, headlines, or hype. The investor who has never withdrawn their crypto is one step away from losing it. The user who has never explored alternatives is one click away from dependence.

This is why understanding the *real* cost of convenience is so important. It's not just about fees or features. It's about *alignment*. Do your habits align with your values? Does your custody model reflect your tolerance for risk, your desire for privacy, your appetite for control? These questions are not philosophical abstractions. They are architectural decisions. Every click, every login, every storage choice is a vote—for a type of future, a type of platform, and a type of user. *Convenience shapes culture.*

The promise of crypto was not that it would be easy. It was that it would be empowering. Empowerment is rarely comfortable. It demands vigilance, literacy, and effort. But the reward is not just security—it is sovereignty. The investor who understands their tools, who audits their own behaviours, who calculates cost not only in dollars but in trust and control, is far better positioned to thrive in a volatile landscape.

Convenience, then, must be redefined. Not as smoothness, but as alignment. A truly convenient setup is not one that hides complexity—it is one that makes your values executable. It allows you to act quickly *because* you've built thoughtfully. It lets you rest confidently *because* you've stored deliberately. That kind of convenience is earned, not purchased. And it never asks you to trade your freedom to save a few clicks.

Exit Plans Before Entry Points

The question isn't whether you can get into a crypto platform. The real question is whether—and how—you can get out. In a market driven by hype and interfaces optimised for onboarding, most investors are seduced by frictionless entry. Very few stop to ask: *What happens when I need to leave?* But that is precisely when clarity matters most. You do not discover a platform's true nature during sign-up. You discover it when you try to withdraw your funds. *Exits are the stress test of trust.* And in crypto, trust isn't what you declare—it's what you design for.

Quiet investors—the ones who survive—and often outperform—tend to ask one question before they click anything: *What's my exit strategy?* This has nothing to do with price predictions or cashing out at the top. It has everything to do with mechanics. Can you withdraw quickly? Can you withdraw fully? Are you subject to delays, fees, thresholds, lockups, or approvals? Do you even know where your funds are being held? These are not small technicalities. They are the difference between having access and simply hoping for it.

Most crypto platforms aren't scams, but many aren't fully solvent either. Liquidity is often contingent, not guaranteed. When you buy crypto on a centralised exchange, you assume that the platform has enough reserves to honour all withdrawals. That assumption is fragile. FTX users discovered this too late. So did Celsius users. And BlockFi's. When withdrawals were paused, the user agreements didn't matter. The app still opened. The balance still displayed. But the exit was sealed. *What looked like ownership was merely exposure.*

Liquidity traps are often subtle. A platform may let you withdraw one asset but not another. You may face delays when converting tokens to fiat. You may be able to trade internally but not externally. Some decentralised platforms restrict exit routes to other ecosystems, making it expensive—or impossible—to bridge assets back to chains you actually use. Others offer "liquidity" through synthetic instruments—wrapped tokens, IOUs, or platform-specific derivatives that can't be redeemed elsewhere. These products work—until they don't. And when confidence collapses, liquidity vanishes in seconds.

Fees are another silent form of exit friction. It's easy to forget how much a withdrawal can cost, especially during high network congestion. A $50 withdrawal fee on a $500 portfolio is a 10% haircut. But more than the absolute number, the deeper issue is unpredictability. If you don't know what it will cost to exit, you don't really have control. That uncertainty becomes paralysing during crises. People delay exits, second-guess decisions, and end up trapped by hesitation. *An exit plan that's unclear in calm markets will become chaotic in volatile ones.*

Then there's the matter of *policy*. Platforms can change withdrawal terms unilaterally. They can introduce KYC requirements after you've already deposited. They can impose delays "for security reasons" or freeze accounts due to "suspicious activity"—a category broad enough to include perfectly legitimate behaviour. This is not a conspiracy theory. It's a legal reality. Most centralised exchanges reserve the right to block or limit access at their discretion. And when they do, support tickets are often met with silence or boilerplate responses. *You are not the customer. You are the counterparty.*

A responsible investor learns to reverse-engineer platforms from their exits. Before making a deposit, ask: Where are the assets custodied? Are withdrawals on-chain or internal transfers? What is the average withdrawal time? Are there fees, limits, or whitelist requirements? Has the platform ever paused withdrawals in the past? Under what conditions? Is there transparency about reserves? Are audits regular and independent? And most importantly: *Can you test the exit before you need it?*

That last step is crucial. Don't wait until panic sets in to discover the boundaries of your access. Make a small withdrawal on day one. Confirm that you control the receiving address. Observe how the platform responds. Does it send a confirmation email? Impose a delay? Require a manual review? These tiny frictions are signals. They reveal how much—or how little—control you actually hold. *If you can't verify an exit today, don't assume it'll be there tomorrow.*

The architecture of exits is also psychological. Many investors don't plan exits because they don't want to believe they'll need one. They're committed to long-term conviction. They trust the project.

They see exit planning as disloyalty. But this is a dangerous conflation. Planning for failure isn't pessimism—it's professionalism. It means thinking through scenarios you hope never occur. It means treating your money with respect, not emotion. *The investor who has rehearsed their exit does not panic. They act.*

There's a larger philosophical shift at play here. In traditional finance, exits are assumed. Banks let you withdraw. Brokerages let you sell. Unless you're under legal restriction, your assets are accessible. Crypto flips that default. There is no "right" to liquidity—only the systems you choose to rely on. Some offer true self-custody and on-chain access. Others give you dashboards that look like control but collapse under pressure. *The test is not how a platform functions during deposits. It's how it behaves when markets stress, networks congest, and sentiment turns.*

Regulatory pressure also plays a role. As governments tighten oversight, many platforms are pre-emptively limiting exits. Stablecoin conversions may be restricted. Cross-border transfers may be flagged. Privacy-enhancing withdrawals may be blocked. These actions may be framed as compliance, but their effect is the same: exit friction increases. And once the precedent is set, it rarely reverses. *Freedom of entry without freedom of exit is not freedom—it's entrapment.*

This is where decentralised infrastructure becomes not just preferable, but essential. Protocols that enable peer-to-peer transfers, decentralised liquidity pools, and self-custodial wallets provide real exits. They are slower. They require more effort. But they honour one of crypto's foundational promises: that you can always walk away. That you can convert your assets, move them, hold them, without asking permission. *That power is only real if you build for it.*

Of course, decentralised exits are not free from risk. Bridges can be exploited. Liquidity can dry up. Interfaces can be complex. But the key difference is *agency*. You control the keys. You sign the transactions. You decide the path. With centralised platforms, you delegate that control. Sometimes that delegation is appropriate. But it should always be conscious. Not assumed. Not defaulted. Not habitual.

A final thought: the best investors don't just know how to exit—they know *when not to enter.* If the exit terms are unclear, the platform is opaque, the history dubious, or the liquidity questionable, the quiet investor stays away. They don't chase every new listing or trend. They don't let FOMO override their protocols. They understand that *entry is optional, but exit is mandatory.* Every asset you acquire becomes a responsibility. Every platform you trust becomes a dependency. And every dependency, left unexamined, becomes a risk.

So ask yourself before you act: *If everything went wrong, could I get out—cleanly, quickly, and fully?* If the answer is anything less than an unambiguous yes, you already know what to do. Or rather, what *not* to do. Because silence at the exit is never just a technical problem. It's a failure of design, of preparation, and of respect—for your capital, your time, and your autonomy. *Plan to leave before you decide to stay.*

Chapter 5
The Big Three – Bitcoin, Ethereum, and the Stablecoin Dilemma

To the casual observer, Bitcoin, Ethereum, and stablecoins often blur together—tickers flashing across an exchange screen, assets to buy, sell, or clutch tight depending on mood and market chatter. Yet behind those charts sit three entirely different blueprints for how value, power, and trust might be organised. They are not merely digital coins. They are arguments—ideological systems embedded in code, each advancing its own vision of money and its role in society.

Bitcoin is the oldest, the slowest, and paradoxically, the most misunderstood. Popular accounts cast it as a bubble, a "digital gold rush," or the convenient villain in environmental debates. But Bitcoin's essence is not speed, nor speculation—it is delay, deliberate and principled. It resists the frantic churn of the present. Its rhythm is slow because it is designed for endurance. To hold Bitcoin with conviction is to reject the culture of instant gratification. It is to place trust in scarcity and integrity rather than in the endless plasticity of fiat. What seems plodding is, in fact, its rebellion. Bitcoin is patience made monetary, and in that patience lies its quiet insurrection.

Ethereum, by contrast, is not primarily a currency at all. If Bitcoin is a citadel, Ethereum is a workshop. It is not built to fossilise principle, but to evolve a platform. What matters is not ETH the token but the ecosystem it animates: decentralised finance, autonomous organisations, tokenised art, on-chain identities. Its genius lies in adaptability, in modularity, in its openness to experiment. To engage with Ethereum properly requires shifting perspective. One doesn't simply "own" ETH as one might own Bitcoin. One participates—by building, governing, transacting—inside a living, shifting operating system. Ethereum is not where wealth rests. It is where infrastructure is being rewritten.

Then there are stablecoins: the workhorses, the bridges, the paradox. Tether, USDC, DAI—they soothe nerves in a stormy market by promising stability, a dollar anchored in code. They provide liquidity, reduce volatility, ease transactions. Yet they also provoke a thorny question: can a decentralised system truly flourish if it pegs itself to centralised money? Stablecoins are convenient, yes, but they tether users psychologically as well as economically to the very fiat systems crypto sought to sidestep. Their design invites constant scrutiny—over collateralisation, blacklisting powers, regulatory choke points. Are they ladders to sovereignty, or just old habits dressed in digital clothes?

Together, these three—Bitcoin, Ethereum, and stablecoins—form the gravitational pull around which much of crypto now orbits. But treating them as interchangeable "exposures" is to miss the deeper truth. They are not the same wager in different wrappers. They are distinct answers to a single, profound question: what kind of system do you believe in? Bitcoin appeals to those who prize permanence. Ethereum attracts those who crave possibility. Stablecoins speak to pragmatists, wary of volatility yet eager for access. None are neutral. To hold them is not just to invest but to align.

This chapter urges you to look beneath the tickers. You will learn why Bitcoin changes slowly—painfully slowly—because slowness is itself its shield. You will follow Ethereum's trajectory beyond the Merge, as it grows from ideological experiment into digital infrastructure. You will probe the machinery of stablecoins, where they create liquidity but also replicate the hierarchies they were meant to escape.

But more than analysis, you'll be asked to turn the lens inward. Why do you hold what you hold? If your only answer is "because it might rise," then perhaps you are not yet playing the same game as these assets are playing. In crypto, allocation is not just a matter of strategy. It is a mirror of identity. A holder who grasps this truth researches differently, holds differently, even sleeps differently.

We inhabit a financial culture addicted to velocity, novelty, yield. Crypto, at its deepest, is not about chasing novelty but about sharpening clarity. This chapter will not whisper predictions of the next rally. Instead, it will offer questions, frameworks, lenses. It will ask whether your portfolio reflects your convictions, your tolerance for risk, your horizon of patience. Because clarity—not noise—is the real asset.

By its end, you will see Bitcoin, Ethereum, and stablecoins not only as tools of finance but as cultural scripts, each with its own grammar. You will recognise whether you hold for utility, for philosophy, or for speculation—and how confusion between them leads to missteps. And perhaps most valuable of all, you will begin to shape a strategy aligned with your life rather than with the fleeting fervour of someone else's feed. That alignment is the true alpha. It steadies not only in euphoria but in the long, unmoving silence of markets.

Bitcoin as Digital Patience

Bitcoin is widely described as volatile, unpredictable, and speculative—but that framing says more about the observer than the asset. To understand Bitcoin solely through the lens of short-term price movements is to miss its deeper cultural proposition. Bitcoin is not a promise of instant wealth; it is a mechanism of delayed gratification. It is a system engineered for those who can wait. Not because waiting is fashionable, but because it's *foundational.* At its core, Bitcoin rewards discipline over impulse, conviction over conformity, and time preference over time pressure. It invites us to ask a much older question, rarely posed in the modern financial world: *What kind of person does this system make me become?*

To see Bitcoin as digital patience is to reframe it not as a tool of speculation but as a social contract with the future. Its fixed supply—hard-coded at 21 million coins—forces a confrontation with scarcity, a concept increasingly abstract in a world of inflationary currencies and central bank intervention. In a fiat environment, money can be created with a keystroke, and the meaning of "saving" has eroded alongside interest rates. Bitcoin reverses this psychological script. It says: *this is all there will ever be.* And by doing so, it reintroduces the logic of limits into an economy addicted to expansion.

The Austrian economic tradition describes this shift in behaviour as a change in *time preference.* High time preference seeks immediate reward. It borrows against tomorrow for pleasure today. Low time preference, by contrast, values the future highly enough to plan for it, to defer consumption, to invest. Bitcoin, as a monetary protocol, encodes this ethos structurally. There is no CEO to inflate supply, no rescue button, no discretionary monetary policy. It is a money system with no central committee and no ability to pander to short-term political interests. The result? *It does not care if you're impatient.*

This disinterest in short-term sentiment is precisely why Bitcoin feels "boring" to those raised on financial adrenaline. It does not offer dividends. It does not yield passive income. It does not cater to traders, nor does it bend to central bank cycles. It simply continues. One block every ten minutes. A halving every four years. An open ledger, visible to all. What appears as rigidity is, in truth, a radical form of clarity. *Bitcoin is valuable because it resists change*, not because it adapts to trends.

Contrast this with legacy financial systems, where constant tweaking is a feature—interest rates manipulated to stimulate consumption, quantitative easing used to paper over crises, and moral hazard baked into the architecture. Fiat systems are reactive. Bitcoin is not. It is immune to popularity contests, indifferent to public relations, and unresponsive to lobbying. It is, in the words of many of its advocates, "antifragile"—strengthening as it survives stress. But this resilience comes at a cost: it requires the user to do something our age finds increasingly difficult—*to wait without reacting.*

Stories abound of early adopters who bought Bitcoin in 2011 or 2013, only to sell during a crash, convinced it had failed. Their error wasn't technical; it was temporal. They couldn't endure the volatility because they lacked a framework for interpreting it. Bitcoin is volatile in the short term because it is maturing in public. It is bootstrapping trust, liquidity, and global infrastructure while constantly under attack from both states and speculators. To hold Bitcoin successfully is not to predict its next move, but to understand that *its value accrues slowly, through persistence and protocol integrity.*

That's why so many of Bitcoin's most committed advocates speak not in months or quarters, but in halvings. They measure time in four-year epochs because that is the pace of the protocol. This perspective is not merely financial—it is philosophical. It mirrors how cultures once thought about stewardship, legacy, and generational wealth. Today's systems optimise for quarterly earnings. Bitcoin asks: *What is your thesis for the next twenty years?*

This temporal reorientation is perhaps Bitcoin's most radical offering. It doesn't just decentralise money; it decentralises *urgency.* In doing so, it threatens the very engines that drive our attention economy. It resists the logic of FOMO, fights the culture of instant commentary, and invites an older ethic—one that values restraint over reaction. It forces investors to confront their own psychology: Can you distinguish volatility from risk? Can you differentiate signal from noise? Can you make peace with stillness in a world of noise?

Even the act of custody—holding your own keys—reinforces this ethic. Unlike traditional financial accounts where banks secure your funds and passwords are reset with a phone call, Bitcoin requires responsibility. If you lose your keys, you lose your coins. This harsh truth is not a bug; it is a mirror. It asks: *Do you want sovereignty, or just access?* Many are drawn to the idea of "freedom" that Bitcoin represents, but few grasp that freedom, in this case, is indistinguishable from accountability.

Bitcoin, then, is not just a network or a number on a screen. It is a filter. It selects for temperament. Those with low time preference tend to stay. Those with high time preference tend to self-sabotage. This is not moralising; it's pattern recognition. In a space where price is often mistaken for signal, patience becomes the rarest form of edge.

Consider the contrast with altcoins and meme tokens that surge and crash within weeks. These assets are engineered to appeal to short attention spans. They gamify finance. They exploit cognitive biases. Bitcoin does the opposite: it is *deliberately unsexy.* There is no marketing team, no brand refresh, no roadmap to dazzle. Its most powerful updates—like Taproot—are barely noticed by the mainstream. And yet, this quiet evolution is the point. *Bitcoin grows like an oak tree, not like a startup.*

This isn't to suggest that Bitcoin is without flaws or blind spots. Its energy use remains contentious, its UX often frustrating, and its governance model—if it can be called that—opaque to newcomers. But these are not symptoms of neglect. They are, in many cases, the result of trade-offs made in service of its core mission: *to be apolitical, permissionless, and unchangeable without overwhelming consensus.* If Bitcoin were easy to modify, it would be easy to co-opt. Its slowness is its shield.

For the thoughtful investor, then, Bitcoin is less a play and more a posture. It asks not "how much can you make?" but "how long can you wait?" It requires a new literacy—not just in cryptography or macroeconomics, but in temperament. This is why the best writing about Bitcoin often reads more like philosophy than finance. It is not just a bet on code; it is a bet on *what kind of world survives when the short-term burns out.*

To hold Bitcoin meaningfully is to express a belief that some things are worth building slowly. It is to reject hyper-financialisation in favour of foundational clarity. It is to say: *I don't need to win quickly, because I understand what I'm aligned with.* That is not just investment strategy. That is *cultural resistance.*

So when someone asks whether Bitcoin is too slow, too boring, too resistant to change—the better question is: *What kind of investor are you becoming?* Because how you relate to Bitcoin is not just a reflection of your asset allocation. It's a reflection of your worldview. And in a world that moves fast and breaks things, the willingness to move slow and protect something *may be the most radical act of all.*

Ethereum: The Operating System of Innovation

To regard Ethereum merely as a cryptocurrency is to mistake the interface for the infrastructure. While headlines track the price of ETH with obsessive frequency—treating it like just another speculative asset—Ethereum is quietly operating as a decentralised engine for software coordination. It is less comparable to gold or stocks than it is to something more ambient, more infrastructural: the internet itself. What TCP/IP did for information exchange,

Ethereum aspires to do for value, governance, and programmable trust. It is not just a digital asset; it is a distributed platform where rules become code, and code becomes law. The sooner one stops treating Ethereum as a line on a chart and starts seeing it as a layer beneath the next wave of digital experiments, the clearer its significance becomes.

Ethereum is best understood not as a product but as a substrate—a permissionless base layer upon which decentralised applications (dApps) can run without relying on central servers or intermediaries. This is a profound departure from traditional software development. Whereas legacy platforms like Apple or Amazon act as gatekeepers, dictating who may build, launch, and monetise apps within their ecosystems, Ethereum offers an open field. There is no central approval process, no App Store politics. Anyone, anywhere, can deploy smart contracts—self-executing code with the autonomy to manage assets, enforce conditions, and coordinate users. This capacity has given rise to an ecosystem that is simultaneously anarchic and astonishingly inventive.

The implications are not theoretical. Ethereum is already powering some of the most consequential experiments in the emerging crypto economy. Consider decentralised finance (DeFi)—a parallel financial system built entirely from open-source protocols. Lending platforms like Aave, decentralised exchanges like Uniswap, and yield aggregators like Yearn Finance are not just products; they are pieces of composable software that interact like digital Lego. A user can borrow against crypto collateral, swap assets, earn interest, or provide liquidity—all without speaking to a banker or filling out a form. The logic of finance is abstracted into programmable contracts. And crucially, the user is not the product; the user is the participant.

This architectural openness extends far beyond financial tools. Ethereum has also become the backbone of non-fungible tokens (NFTs), which—despite their speculative hype—represent a novel form of digital ownership. An NFT is not merely a JPEG; it is a cryptographic certificate of uniqueness. It can encode authorship, provenance, royalties, and access. Artists can now release limited digital works, musicians can sell token-gated albums, and communities can form around digital artefacts whose value is not centrally determined but socially negotiated. Whether one sees NFTs as art, identity, or economic coordination, they represent an entirely new design space—one that Ethereum made possible.

Equally transformative are decentralised autonomous organisations (DAOs), which use Ethereum smart contracts to formalise group decision-making. Instead of a corporate board or NGO hierarchy, DAOs encode governance into code. Proposals are submitted on-chain, votes are tallied transparently, and funds can be disbursed automatically. This isn't Silicon Valley managerialism dressed in crypto clothing—it is a genuine experiment in software-native governance. Some DAOs manage treasuries worth millions; others coordinate artistic collectives, research funds, or activist campaigns. What they share is a belief that coordination itself can be reimagined—not by trusting institutions, but by trusting transparent code and collective incentives.

It would be a mistake, however, to interpret Ethereum's openness as utopianism. The network faces real challenges—scalability chief among them. As activity has surged, transaction fees (gas) have often spiked, pricing out casual users and raising questions about Ethereum's accessibility. Solutions are underway—Layer 2 rollups, sharding, and protocol upgrades like Ethereum 2.0—but the ecosystem is evolving in real time, with the risks and frictions that come with it. There are also cultural tensions: between developers who favour radical decentralisation and investors seeking predictability; between maximalists who view Ethereum as the only viable smart contract platform and pluralists who see a multi-chain future. Ethereum is not a monolith. It is a living system with factions, trade-offs, and ideological fault lines.

This dynamism is precisely what makes Ethereum more than a static technology. It is *cultural infrastructure.* To choose Ethereum is not just to back a protocol; it is to align with a set of values—openness, experimentation, resistance to gatekeeping. But these values are not without cost. There is no customer support hotline, no final arbiter of disputes, no safety net for lost keys. With sovereignty comes risk. Ethereum demands fluency, vigilance, and an ongoing willingness to learn. Yet for many, this friction is a feature, not a bug. It is what makes the ecosystem fertile for invention. *Constraint breeds creativity.*

Look beyond Ethereum's market cap or the price of ETH, and you will find a dense social fabric: developers maintaining client software, researchers debating protocol upgrades, DAOs voting on treasury allocations, artists launching on-chain exhibitions. Ethereum is not just code. It is a community of coordination. Unlike Bitcoin, which famously aspires to ossify, Ethereum embraces change—though with an awareness that change must be consensus-driven and carefully staged. It is both adaptive and deliberate. Every upgrade, every improvement proposal (EIP), must be rigorously debated, tested, and implemented without central control. This is not agility in the startup sense; it is *collaborative evolution at scale.*

Critically, Ethereum invites us to reframe our understanding of trust. Whereas Bitcoin removes trust from human actors by enforcing rules through immutability, Ethereum enables *programmable trust.* The goal is not to eliminate discretion but to modularise it. You don't have to trust a bank—you trust an audited contract. You don't need to trust a CEO—you vote on governance. This modular trust is especially valuable in domains where coordination is difficult: global remittances, peer-to-peer insurance, data marketplaces. The implications reach far beyond finance.

To participate meaningfully in Ethereum, then, is to engage with it not merely as an investment, but as an operating system for digital life. Just as early internet users built websites, blogs, and open-source tools—not to get rich, but to participate in a new paradigm—Ethereum builders are creating mechanisms for ownership, community, and self-determination. To reduce this to "number go up" is to miss the revolution. Ethereum is where the future of programmable coordination is being prototyped in public view.

That does not mean every project will succeed. Many will fail. Some are scams, others are sincere but premature. The permissionless nature of Ethereum means that quality control is decentralised. Discernment becomes essential. There is no trusted brand, no due diligence department. The investor, the user, the builder—all must develop critical literacy. But again, this is a feature: *the user is not insulated from the system.* They are entangled with it. And in a culture where centralised platforms make billions while users own nothing, Ethereum flips the script: it gives ownership to participants, not just shareholders.

Understanding Ethereum, then, requires an expanded lens. It is not a company, a product, or a single narrative. It is an evolving toolkit for rethinking digital interaction. It is a playground for new economic structures. It is a bet on composability over control, on transparency over trust-me, and on coordination without coercion. That it is still early—and imperfect—does not diminish its significance. It simply reminds us that the infrastructure of the future is still being built.

For those navigating the crypto landscape, seeing Ethereum as a mere asset is insufficient. It is more accurate to think of it as *a terrain.* A digital landscape where new rules can be written, tested, and deployed without permission. It is messy, complex, and, at times, overwhelming. But within that mess lies possibility—the kind of possibility that only emerges when systems are open, incentives are aligned, and imagination is not gated by hierarchy.

Ethereum may never be finished. That is its strength. It is not a product to be shipped. It is *an invitation to build.* And in a world increasingly shaped by opaque algorithms and centralised authority, such invitations are rare—and worth noticing.

Stablecoins: Anchors or Illusions?

At first glance, stablecoins appear to offer the best of both worlds: the familiarity of fiat with the flexibility of crypto. Pegged to a stable asset—most commonly the US dollar—they promise predictability in a notoriously volatile environment. But beneath this surface calm lies a deeper tension: are stablecoins truly bridges to a decentralised future, or are they just comfort blankets that smuggle legacy risks into new architecture? Investors often mistake stability for safety, but in the case of stablecoins, *psychological stability may obscure structural fragility.*

To understand why stablecoins matter, it helps to start with what they solve. Volatility has long been the Achilles' heel of cryptocurrencies. For new users, the prospect of holding an asset that might gain or lose 20% in a week can be psychologically jarring. For developers, pricing services or contracts in fluctuating currencies is a design nightmare. Stablecoins were introduced as a practical remedy: a unit of account that wouldn't swing wildly in value. This predictability became foundational for many decentralised applications. It enabled borrowing and lending protocols, priced NFT sales, and served as a liquidity base in decentralised exchanges. In many ways, stablecoins became *the rails on which the crypto economy quietly ran.*

But this calm exterior masks a sharp divergence in implementation. Not all stablecoins are created equal. Broadly, there are three main designs: fiat-collateralised, crypto-collateralised, and algorithmic. Each comes with trade-offs that are more than technical—they are philosophical.

Fiat-collateralised stablecoins, like USDT (Tether) and USDC (issued by Circle), are backed by reserves held in traditional financial institutions. These coins claim to be redeemable 1:1 for actual dollars, creating a perception of reliability. Yet this architecture reintroduces the very intermediaries that crypto set out to avoid. Users may be transacting in tokens, but the system behind them still hinges on banks, regulators, auditors, and corporate governance. Trust is not removed—it's relocated. And in this relocation lies the risk: a fiat-backed stablecoin is only as stable as the solvency, transparency, and legal compliance of the issuing entity. When confidence wavers, even for a moment—as it did with Tether during its reserve controversies—markets react sharply. *The peg may hold, but the faith can falter.*

Crypto-collateralised stablecoins, like DAI, attempt a more decentralised approach. Instead of trusting banks, users lock up crypto assets in smart contracts to mint new coins. The system is designed to be over-collateralised—often by 150% or more—to account for market swings. While more aligned with decentralised values, these models introduce their own challenges. Price drops can trigger liquidations, leading to cascading effects. Managing collateral ratios becomes a game of constant vigilance. Moreover, many "decentralised" stablecoins end up relying on centralised price oracles, governance votes, and liquidity incentives. They may be more transparent, but they are not immune to complexity or failure.

The third category—algorithmic stablecoins—aims to maintain a peg through market incentives and supply adjustments, rather than explicit collateral. These are elegant in theory, fragile in practice. The collapse of TerraUSD (UST) in 2022 was a stark demonstration. When confidence in its algorithmic model cracked, it triggered a death spiral that wiped out tens of billions in value. The lesson was brutal but necessary: *an asset cannot be stable by rhetoric alone.* Algorithmic pegs require not just belief but sustained equilibrium between incentives, liquidity, and market behaviour. Once that balance slips, recovery is near-impossible.

What all three models reveal is that stability is not a binary trait—it is an emergent property. And that property is only as robust as the mechanisms, incentives, and governance underpinning it. Stablecoins are not static instruments; they are dynamic systems, constantly negotiating between confidence and control. Understanding them requires not just technical literacy but conceptual clarity. What are you actually trusting when you hold a stablecoin? Is it the asset? The issuer? The smart contract? The market?

This question becomes even more pressing when considering stablecoins' expanding role in global finance. In countries facing currency devaluation, dollar-backed stablecoins have become a lifeline. In Argentina, Venezuela, Nigeria, and Turkey, citizens increasingly turn to USDC or USDT to preserve savings or conduct trade. What began as a crypto-native innovation has now become a de facto shadow dollar system. But this very adoption reveals the geopolitical entanglements of stablecoins. If a stablecoin issuer is pressured by regulators, sanctioned by a government, or compromised by legal action, users in far-off countries could find themselves cut off. The asset may be decentralised, but the infrastructure is not. *Convenience brings centralisation in through the back door.*

Privacy is another area where stablecoins raise critical concerns. Most fiat-backed stablecoins maintain compliance with KYC (Know Your Customer) and AML (Anti-Money Laundering) regulations. In practice, this means that every wallet holding or transacting in USDC could be subject to surveillance, blacklisting, or account freezing. This isn't hypothetical—Circle has frozen addresses before. For those who believe crypto should enable financial autonomy, this raises a disquieting question: *are stablecoins Trojan horses for the very systems they sought to sidestep?*

At the same time, it would be simplistic to write off stablecoins entirely. For many users, they are not ideological tools but practical instruments. A trader needs liquidity. A borrower needs predictable interest rates. A remittance sender needs stability across borders. The usability of crypto is enhanced when value can be transferred without volatility shocks. In this sense, stablecoins are *functional bridges*—they make it possible to move between fiat and crypto worlds without constant recalibration.

But bridges can be bottlenecks. And they can collapse. The danger is not just technical—it is psychological. Stablecoins lull users into a false sense of permanence. They appear as neutral instruments, when in fact they are deeply political. They appear risk-free, when in fact their risk is simply deferred or displaced. They appear simple, when they are in fact embedded in complex and contested systems. *The illusion of simplicity is the risk.*

This becomes especially salient for long-term investors. If you are parking funds in stablecoins between trades, that may be a rational tactical move. But if you are holding them as long-term stores of value, you are making a different bet—one on regulatory stability, counterparty trust, and dollar supremacy. That may be acceptable for some portfolios, but it must be acknowledged for what it is. Every asset is a thesis. Every position reflects a worldview. Stablecoins are no exception.

The question, then, is not whether stablecoins are good or bad. It is whether they are *understood.* If you use a stablecoin, ask: who controls it? What backs it? What happens if the peg fails, if redemptions are halted, if legal action targets the issuer? What rights do you have?

What exit paths exist? These are not hypothetical concerns. They are due diligence questions—questions that responsible investors must ask before confusing comfort with security.

Ironically, the very stability of stablecoins makes them dangerous to ignore. Because they seem uneventful, they encourage complacency. But crypto is not a realm where quiet equals safety. Sometimes, the most serene-looking instruments are hiding the most leverage. A rational investor does not equate psychological comfort with systemic resilience. They look under the hood.

Ultimately, stablecoins are mirrors. They reflect not only market needs but cultural assumptions. Do we crave predictability so much that we are willing to trade sovereignty for it? Do we believe in decentralisation until it becomes inconvenient? Are we trying to escape fiat systems—or rebuild them in new packaging?

These are not academic questions. They cut to the core of what crypto is trying to be. Stablecoins reveal a paradox at the heart of the ecosystem: *to move fast, we rely on stable tools; but those tools, in turn, may re-anchor us to the very systems we sought to disrupt.* Whether that's a feature or a flaw depends on your goals, your time horizon, and your appetite for ambiguity.

Stablecoins are neither saviours nor saboteurs. They are scaffolding—temporary, provisional, contingent. Use them with eyes open, not hearts closed. Understand what you hold, why you hold it, and what trade-offs you are implicitly accepting. Because in crypto, as in life, *there is no such thing as a neutral bridge.* Only directions. Only values. Only choices.

Knowing What You Hold—and Why

Crypto's openness is its invitation, and its trap. With near-instant access to thousands of tokens, projects, and protocols, the modern investor can own slivers of a decentralised exchange, a metaverse land parcel, an AI prediction market, and a tokenised bottle of whisky—all before breakfast. The question is no longer *can* you hold an asset. The question is: *should* you? And more precisely: *why* do you?

Most crypto portfolios are constructed reactively. A tweet triggers curiosity. A price chart spikes. A friend mentions a "hidden gem." You act before you understand, and rationalise after the fact. This is not investing. It's narrative grazing—an unstructured, emotion-led accumulation of exposure masquerading as strategy. The cost isn't just monetary. It's cognitive. Over time, the portfolio you build reflects not your convictions but your confusion.

Clarity in crypto is radical. It requires saying no to most things, not yes to everything. It means refusing to chase every new token or trend without understanding the core thesis behind it. To know what you hold, you must know what problem the asset claims to solve, how it attempts to solve it, and why that solution is superior to alternatives. And beyond the asset's logic, you must be equally clear on your own. *What role does this token play in your financial vision? What horizon are you measuring? What risk are you accepting?*

Start with Bitcoin. If you hold it, why? Is it a hedge against inflation? A decentralised store of value? A protest against monetary debasement? Or is it just "number go up"? Each frame implies different behaviours. If you see Bitcoin as a long-term store of value, then short-term price movements are noise. You don't need to check daily charts. You don't panic sell on dips. You size your position conservatively and leave it alone. But if you hold Bitcoin because you hope to sell it when it doubles next month, you're trading, not investing—and you should be honest about that.

Now consider Ethereum. Do you view it as a platform for innovation, akin to owning digital infrastructure? Are you betting on its growing role in powering DeFi, NFTs, DAOs, and more? Or is it just a proxy for crypto market health? If your belief is in Ethereum's ecosystem, you might allocate more over time, treat ETH as equity in an emergent economy, and support its evolution through staking or governance. If your understanding is vague—if you hold ETH simply because "everyone else does"—you're vulnerable to disillusionment when the narrative shifts or competitors gain ground.

Then there are stablecoins. If you hold USDC or USDT, what's your reasoning? Are you using them to exit volatility temporarily? Are they parking spots between trades? Are you using them for yield? Each motive has different risk implications. A parking spot must be safe and liquid. A yield instrument must be vetted for counterparty risk. A long-term holding implies trust in the issuer and the peg. If you haven't asked yourself these questions, your use of stablecoins may be exposing you to hidden vulnerabilities—especially when regulation, depegging events, or blacklisting can render stablecoins unstable overnight.

The same applies to smaller-cap tokens and experimental assets. Do you understand the tokenomics? The supply schedule? The governance model? The real user adoption? If your portfolio includes a DAO token, what's the DAO's mandate? Does it generate revenue? Do token holders control something meaningful? Or is it just a speculative placeholder for hopes yet unrealised?

Knowing what you hold means seeing through the *surface narrative.* Many crypto assets market themselves with polished websites, pseudo-academic whitepapers, and buzzword-heavy roadmaps. But real value lies beneath that gloss. You need to understand who's building the protocol, who's using it, how it sustains itself, and what assumptions its success depends on. If any of those pillars are unclear, your position is not grounded in understanding—it's rooted in hope.

Asset allocation is more than percentages. It's a mirror of your beliefs, your goals, and your risk appetite. If 70% of your portfolio is in micro-cap tokens you couldn't explain to a friend, what does that say about your priorities? Are you chasing outsized returns? Do you secretly believe you missed Bitcoin and want to find "the next one"? Do you find comfort in action even when the action lacks structure?

The noise of the crypto market makes clarity rare. Social media incentivises hot takes over deep thought. Influencers speak in absolutes. Trends flip in weeks. But *long-term wealth is built on clear, reasoned conviction.* You don't need to hold everything. You need to hold what aligns with your strategy. And that strategy must be personal. It must fit your life, your timeline, and your temperament—not someone else's.

This is especially true during bear markets. When prices fall and hype evaporates, the only thing that remains is clarity—or regret. If you understood why you held an asset, you're more likely to endure its drawdowns. If you bought in ignorance, panic will follow. Every correction is a test of your thesis. And if you didn't have one, the test will be painful.

The antidote to confusion is intentionality. Before buying any asset, ask yourself: What problem does this solve? Why do I believe this solution will endure? What am I willing to risk for this belief? What time horizon makes sense? What would make me change my mind? If you cannot answer these questions, the asset may not belong in your portfolio—yet.

This clarity also protects you from over-diversification. While spreading risk is wise, owning dozens of unrelated tokens you don't understand is not diversification. It's dilution. Every position you hold should earn its place. It should reflect a distinct thesis. If multiple tokens serve the same function or track the same market, consider consolidating. *Simplicity sharpens focus. Clarity compounds over time.*

Ultimately, this is about financial sovereignty. In traditional investing, you can outsource conviction to fund managers or analysts. In crypto, that luxury is rare. You are your own research desk. Your own risk officer. Your own fiduciary. That reality demands maturity. It demands saying "no" more than "yes." It demands slowing down when the market speeds up.

Crypto rewards clarity. Not instantly, but inevitably. The investors who endure are not those who guess correctly most often—they're the ones who understand deeply, act deliberately, and revisit their assumptions with humility. Knowing what you hold is not a checklist item. It's a posture. A habit. A discipline.

As this market matures, that discipline will become a competitive advantage. It will separate the signal from the noise, the builders from the speculators, the investors from the tourists. And for you, the reader, it starts now—not with your next trade, but with your next question. What do I hold? Why do I hold it? What does it say about me?

Because a crypto portfolio is more than numbers on a screen. It is a reflection of how clearly you think, how well you understand, and how consciously you choose. Make every asset in it earn your trust. And make your trust a scarce, valuable thing.

Chapter 6
Safety Is a Skill, Not a Setting

The most perilous assumption a novice investor can make in crypto is to believe that security is a switch—something you flip on once and leave humming in the background. A browser plug-in, a toggle inside an app, a hardware wallet stashed in a drawer. But security in this realm is not a product to be bought. It is a discipline, a posture. Not a checklist item, but a mindset. In traditional finance, responsibility for safety is outsourced; in crypto, it is inherited. Like it or not, it lands squarely on you.

Blockchain's architecture hands you ownership directly. But ownership without vigilance is not freedom—it is exposure. The very infrastructure that lets you move money without intermediaries also strips away the safety nets they provided. No customer service line, no password reset, no appeal if you err. And while cryptography underpins the system, it is not algorithms alone that keep you safe. It is your habits, your attention, the judgement calls you make in moments of uncertainty. Security in crypto is behavioural before it is technical.

Most newcomers misjudge this. They imagine hackers as shadowy figures hammering at firewalls with lines of code. In practice, compromises far more often begin with a private message, a fake support agent, a poisoned link dressed as opportunity. Attackers rarely need to outwit mathematics. They need only to outwit you. And they are resourceful, patient, inventive. Which means your strongest shield is not suspicion for its own sake but the ability to recognise patterns—signals that something is off. To see the "urgent offer" as bait, the forced timeline as manipulation, the generosity as camouflage.

Scammers operate not with force but with mimicry. They borrow trust. They pose as team members, clone brand accounts, play on emotions: greed, fear, the dread of missing out. One lapse of attention, a single distracted click, can undo years of careful saving. Yet the reverse also holds: a few ingrained habits, repeated steadily, can protect you more reliably than any expensive device.

This is the social layer of security—arguably the most important, and certainly the least taught. No system is sturdier than the person who operates it. Phishing works not because encryption breaks, but because people wish to be helpful, or they fear delay, or they mistake familiarity for authenticity. Which is why some of the most powerful upgrades to your security are psychological. To see urgency as a pressure tactic. To pause rather than comply. Trust, in this world, should be rationed and earned, not handed out casually.

Consider the string of social engineering attacks that compromised high-profile Twitter accounts, NFT holders, even developer collectives. These were not feats of cryptographic wizardry. They were simple breaches of human trust—an email from a lookalike domain, a Discord role given to a wolf in sheep's clothing, a Google Form coaxing seed phrases from the unwary. Not high-tech assaults, but low-tech deceits that succeed precisely because they are ordinary.

True security does not rest on fear. Fear paralyses. Awareness sharpens. The call here is not to paranoia but to vigilance. There is a difference between healthy caution and debilitating suspicion. You don't need to retreat from communities or scan every interaction with forensic intensity. But you do need personal protocols—rules you live by, not just the ones embedded in code.

This is where digital hygiene matters—not as an afterthought but as a foundation. Do you rely on a password manager? Where is your seed phrase stored, and who could stumble upon it? Have you rehearsed your recovery process before you must use it? Do you update software, enable two-factor authentication, compartmentalise your accounts? These details may seem mundane. They are not. They are the quiet scaffolding of resilience.

The aim is not to erase risk. That is impossible. The aim is to carve out a margin of safety: habits that create time, clarity, and options when the unexpected happens. And it will happen. Devices fail, passwords are forgotten, exchanges freeze withdrawals. In such moments, you want systems already in place—backups tested, permissions pruned, exits rehearsed.

Perhaps most underrated is instinct. The gut, long dismissed as fear or doubt, is often wisdom in disguise. Fear has been treated in crypto as weakness, a lack of conviction. But when examined, fear is not the enemy; it is a signal. Pause before clicking. Re-read before signing. Delay before committing funds. The trick is to tell the difference between fear as noise and fear as intelligence. Harnessed well, it becomes foresight.

This chapter will not drown you in tools or settings. It will teach you to think like someone who is hard to compromise. To read signals early, to expect that every request might carry risk, to respond deliberately rather than react hastily. Security, at its core, is compound interest in behavioural form. Attention over automation. Curiosity over complacency. Patience over impulse.

As crypto grows, the field will only become richer—for builders, yes, but also for those who exploit. The ones who last will not simply be early adopters or lucky sellers. They will be the ones who kept hold of their keys, who ignored the poisoned link, who remembered fundamentals when frenzy took hold.

You can be among them. Not by accident, but by design. This chapter shows you how.

Recognizing Red Flags in Real Time

The most expensive mistakes in crypto are rarely made through ignorance of technology. They're made through misplaced trust. Not in code, but in people, platforms, and promises that appear credible—right until they vanish. The modern scam is not a brute-force attack. It's a precision game of psychology, timing, and familiarity. And the only way to defend yourself is to cultivate a skill that can't be automated: *pattern recognition.*

The cryptocurrency space is a breeding ground for deception precisely because it is new, fast-moving, and often opaque. That volatility isn't limited to price—it applies to information, identity, and intent. Opportunists know that confusion is currency. They trade on your unfamiliarity with the norms. They speak the language of innovation to hide exploitation. And they look exactly like everyone else: clean branding, active Twitter feeds, polished websites, and Discord communities with thousands of members. *Fraud doesn't wear a mask—it wears a logo.*

A red flag is never red until you've seen it waved enough times to know. That's why pattern recognition must be built before the danger appears, not after the damage is done. Consider how many scams have operated in plain sight, unflagged, because the packaging mimicked legitimate innovation. From the rug-pulls of anonymous NFT projects to elaborate token launch scams disguised as DeFi opportunities, the technique is always the same: appear cutting-edge, promise outsized returns, and establish social proof quickly. If you can generate enough fear of missing out (FOMO), the crowd will silence its doubts.

But genuine projects rarely shout. They don't pressure. They don't rush you to connect your wallet or click airdrop links or "verify" yourself through Google Forms. Scams rely on urgency as a substitute for legitimacy. *If someone wants you to act before you can think, they don't want you to think.* Pause there.

Let's examine the anatomy of a contemporary crypto scam. It usually begins with authority theatre. The scammer impersonates someone respected—perhaps a known founder, an admin in a community, or even a brand partnership. Their name might be misspelled by a single character, their Twitter handle altered subtly, their messages filled with familiar syntax. From there, they establish context. "We're selecting a small group of early supporters…" or "This is a limited beta for trusted members…" The bait is always exclusivity. The trap is always trust. One wrong click, one fake link, and your assets are no longer yours.

These attacks don't only affect newcomers. Developers, influencers, investors with years in the space have all been compromised because of one core mistake: they treated familiarity as authentication. But in Web3, *identity is programmable.* Anyone can copy a name, clone a smart contract, mirror a website's CSS. The question is not whether something looks familiar, but whether it *verifies*. And the only way to verify is not with intuition alone—but with verification tools, domain scrutiny, and a strong default of scepticism.

A real-world case illustrates this vividly. In 2021, a fake version of the Uniswap exchange interface was deployed under a nearly identical domain name. The smart contract itself was malicious. Users who connected wallets and approved token swaps had their entire balances drained. Many of these users were seasoned DeFi participants who simply didn't notice a missing letter in the URL. They trusted their browser history more than their eyes. And the browser didn't flag the site—because the SSL certificate was real. *Authenticity is no longer a design feature—it must be a conscious check.*

Scams are increasingly layered with social engineering. Consider Discord or Telegram communities. A new user joins a group to ask a question about a wallet or transaction. Within minutes, they receive a "helpful" direct message from a fake support agent, offering to troubleshoot. The fake agent might use real logos, scripted language, and a convincing tone. The user is guided to a fake support portal, asked for their seed phrase "for verification," and within seconds, their funds disappear. This is not a high-tech hack. It is a confidence trick. And its success relies entirely on the illusion of helpfulness.

To resist these tactics, you must internalise a few principles. First: *no legitimate service will ever ask for your private key or seed phrase*. Ever. Not for troubleshooting, not for "verification," not even to help recover funds. Second: *DMs are not support channels.* Treat unsolicited messages in crypto spaces as inherently suspect. Third: *urgency is a tactic, not a signal of opportunity*. Anything worth doing in crypto is still worth doing slowly.

A different class of red flag comes in the form of too-good-to-be-true returns. Yield farms offering 1,000% APY. New tokens promising 10x in a week. Smart contracts "guaranteeing" price floors. These aren't projects. They're bait. And the only reason they persist is because the line between risk and scam is sometimes intentionally blurred. Some protocols are not scams—but they are designed to fail eventually. Their economics are unsustainable, their liquidity is shallow, or their incentive structures reward early exit at everyone else's expense. *Not all failures are fraud—but most frauds are built to fail.*

The best defence is not to avoid all risk, but to ask better questions. Who controls the smart contract? Is it upgradeable? Is there an audit—and is the audit recent, independent, and transparent? What are the tokenomics, and who holds most of the supply? Are the team members public, and are their reputations verifiable beyond a LinkedIn page? *Security starts where curiosity begins.*

Even more dangerous than scams are *pseudo-legitimate ecosystems* that operate in moral grey zones. Projects that collect user data under the banner of decentralisation. Platforms that hold your funds but don't disclose where or how. Exchanges that offer instant access but implement withdrawal delays when markets crash. These entities may not steal your funds, but they erode your sovereignty. And over time, this erosion is more dangerous than any one-time scam. *Deception wrapped in utility is still deception.*

The challenge, then, is to cultivate not just vigilance, but *pattern memory*. To train yourself to notice patterns of manipulation: language that plays on urgency, authority that lacks proof, interfaces that demand before they explain. You are not just clicking links—you are managing exposure. Every interaction is a trade-off between convenience and caution. And your future self depends on how often you choose the latter.

To build real-world instincts, start small. Create a mental checklist: Was this invitation solicited? Do I know this sender from a trusted source? Does the site use HTTPS and match the official domain? Has the smart contract been verified and discussed by others I trust? Have I paused before approving any transaction, especially one that grants "unlimited spend" access to my tokens? These micro-rituals compound. They become second nature. And in a landscape where traps are often invisible, *second nature is your greatest firewall.*

There is a deeper lesson here, beyond fraud prevention. Pattern recognition in crypto is not just about spotting scams—it's about reading power structures. Understanding who benefits from your engagement. Knowing how value is extracted, and by whom.

Spotting red flags is the beginning of discernment, not the end of it. It helps you not only protect yourself—but align yourself with projects that respect you as a participant, not just a target.

And perhaps this is where the maturity of the investor meets the maturity of the ecosystem. The early days of crypto were wild and lawless—but they also taught us something vital: *trust is the only true currency in a decentralised world.* If you hand it out cheaply, it will cost you dearly. But if you protect it, question it, and demand transparency before participation, it will serve you longer than any token ever could.

This chapter doesn't promise that you'll never be targeted again. You will be. Repeatedly. But you'll see it coming sooner. You'll click less, question more, and act slower. And in crypto, *slower is safer.* Because the red flags are there—you just have to teach your eyes to see them before it's too late.

The Social Layer of Security

The greatest vulnerabilities in cryptocurrency do not live in smart contracts or wallets. They live in people. Human behaviour—predictable, emotional, and at times careless—remains the single largest attack surface in digital finance. It is rarely the code that fails first. It is trust. The lesson is unambiguous and brutal: the weakest link in your crypto security stack is not software—it's social.

The myth of cybercrime often begins with the image of a lone hacker cracking through layers of encryption, buried in terminal commands and blinking servers. But this cinematic portrayal obscures the reality. Most breaches occur not through technical wizardry but through persuasion. Not brute force, but manipulation. Not zero-days, but human error. A simple message, a fake form, an urgent request from a familiar face—that's all it takes to dismantle months or even years of diligent asset protection. *Security, in practice, is a social skill before it is a technical one.*

The cryptocurrency world, with its culture of pseudonymity, decentralised access, and high-value transactions, is uniquely fertile ground for social engineering. The very features that make the ecosystem exciting—open communication channels, peer-to-peer engagement, fast-moving communities—also make it exquisitely vulnerable to manipulation. In such an environment, the attacker doesn't need to understand blockchain; they need to understand *you*.

Consider a chilling example: in early 2022, a senior employee at a leading DeFi protocol received a direct message via Telegram. It appeared to come from a colleague. The tone was familiar. The context seemed appropriate. The request was simple: to review a shared document. Without much thought, the employee clicked the link. Unbeknownst to them, the document hosted malicious code. Their credentials were compromised. Minutes later, the protocol's treasury was emptied of over $10 million. No firewall triggered. No alert sounded. The gateway had been human, not digital. *It wasn't a hack—it was an invitation.*

Direct messages are the most common attack vector in the social layer. Discord, Telegram, Twitter—each provides easy and near-instant access to targets. The attacker's first move is always the same: impersonate legitimacy. Fake profiles, copied avatars, mirrored bios, and spoofed usernames create a facade of authenticity. Then comes the "ask"—often phrased as support, collaboration, or urgency. The deception works because the target wants it to be true. They want help. They want opportunity. They want clarity. And that desire overrides scepticism.

Phishing, while well-known, continues to evolve in sophistication. Gone are the days of broken English and clumsy designs. Today's phishing campaigns mimic legitimate platforms down to the pixel. Domains are typosquatted—uniswap[dot]com becomes uniswap[dot]co. Login pages are cloned. Wallet integrations are scripted to behave identically. The user is drawn into a simulation so convincing that even seasoned investors fail to spot the difference. One misplaced click, one hasty seed phrase entry, and the damage is irreversible.

But the most damaging attacks often rely not on anonymity, but intimacy. They target insiders. Employees. Community managers. Advisors. These are people whose reputations carry weight, whose permissions grant access, and whose lapses cascade. Attackers build relationships over time, groom their targets through conversation, familiarity, even praise. Eventually, they introduce an exploit—masked as a shared link, an urgent request, a new tool to try. This is not just phishing. It is *pretexting*—constructing a believable narrative that elicits cooperation. The longer it's built, the less suspicious it seems. By the time the victim acts, the trust feels earned.

Understanding this dynamic forces a shift in how we think about security. It is no longer enough to encrypt, backup, and verify. One must *communicate defensively*. Assume any unsolicited message is potentially malicious. Create private channels for internal coordination. Use out-of-band verification for sensitive actions. If someone asks you to click, connect, or confirm—especially under pressure—pause. Validate their identity through a secondary method. Treat familiarity as a vulnerability, not a safeguard.

The structure of crypto communities often amplifies risk. DAOs, for instance, are governed by token-weighted voting, coordinated over public channels. This transparency is valuable for accountability, but dangerous when exploited. Attackers monitor these discussions, identify influential participants, and craft targeted social engineering campaigns. The more decentralised the governance, the more diffuse the responsibility. And in such systems, *the attacker needs only one weak node to compromise the network*.

Real-world examples are uncomfortably common. In one DAO-focused Discord, a user impersonating a known developer distributed a fake "governance tool" to community members. The tool prompted wallet permissions under the guise of enabling cross-chain voting. Several members lost five-figure sums. The impersonator was banned, but the funds were unrecoverable. The lesson was harsh: even governance infrastructure—designed for democratic participation—can be weaponised through trust.

This is not an argument for paranoia. It is an argument for *operational maturity*. For treating every interaction with the awareness that digital identity is fluid, easily mimicked, and often weaponised. For educating teams, communities, and users not just on how to use wallets or navigate protocols, but on how to *recognise manipulation in real time.* Security is not static. It is behavioural.

One powerful protective measure is *the rule of deliberate delay.* Make it a habit to never act on a request—especially one involving private keys, permissions, or financial movement—without a time buffer. Scams thrive in urgency. Patience dissolves their power. Delay introduces space for validation, reflection, and verification. In a space built on speed, slowing down is often the wisest move.

Another essential shift is to distribute responsibility. Most successful breaches occur in environments with concentrated authority. A single admin account. A single gatekeeper. A single private key. The more power any one person holds, the more catastrophic their compromise. Instead, use multisig wallets, team-based approvals, and tiered access structures. *Make it harder to do damage alone—even to yourself.*

This mindset also requires new rituals. Teach team members to read URLs carefully. To check for browser certificate warnings. To hover before they click. To assume that if something seems too smooth, too fast, too seamless, it may be suspect. These behaviours are small, but together they form a psychological firewall—one that is far more resilient than any hardware device alone.

We must also acknowledge a subtle but critical reality: many users are embarrassed when they are socially engineered. They fear ridicule, judgement, or loss of credibility. This creates a silence that protects the attacker. We need to shift this culture. Breach disclosure should be encouraged, not punished. Every attack is an opportunity to strengthen group awareness. Shame is a weapon for the attacker. Transparency is the antidote.

Ultimately, the social layer of security is not about distrusting everyone. It's about *earning trust slowly, and revoking it quickly.* It's about cultivating a defensive posture that sees through charm, confidence, and perceived familiarity. It's about recognising that Web3 is not only a technical shift—it is a behavioural one. If we fail to adapt at the human level, no protocol upgrade will save us.

The future of security will not be written in lines of code alone. It will be forged in habits, shaped by vigilance, and maintained through shared norms of cautious engagement. In this space, your biggest exposure is not your private key—it is your willingness to assume good intent without verification.

Your eyes, not your wallet, are your first line of defence. Train them well.

Practicing Digital Hygiene

Security in cryptocurrency is often mistaken for the tools you use. But it's not your hardware wallet that keeps you safe—it's the behaviour with which you use it. In the digital asset world, where a single compromised keystroke can equate to irreversible financial loss, *habits matter more than hardware.* This chapter is not about buying another device, app, or subscription. It's about *operationalising discipline.* Security begins not with the latest gadget, but with how you act when no one is watching.

The crypto ecosystem offers no customer support hotline, no forgotten password reset, and no central authority to petition if something goes wrong. That sovereignty is liberating—but also unforgiving. Safety is earned through repetition, not reassurance. And that means building a mental framework in which basic actions become protective reflexes. Most losses in the space don't come from black swan events; they come from avoidable slippage in behaviour. Digital hygiene is not paranoia. It's professionalism.

Start with the obvious—but often neglected: the device. The endpoint through which you interact with wallets, exchanges, and protocols is your first and most frequent risk vector. And yet, many users still treat their phones and laptops like they're interchangeable with general-purpose browsing. If you use the same machine for crypto transactions and casual browsing—YouTube, torrents, pop-ups, social media—you've already introduced unnecessary risk. A compromised browser extension or phishing ad doesn't need to target your assets directly; it just needs to sit silently until you log in to MetaMask.

A dedicated device—used exclusively for crypto-related actions—is not a luxury; it's a line of defence. If that's not possible, hard segregation via user profiles, secure browsers (e.g. Brave or hardened Firefox), and strict plugin discipline can offer a partial safeguard. Antivirus and firewall tools are table stakes, not advanced strategies. But these are the *starting conditions*, not the full game. Even pristine hardware won't save you from bad habits.

Let's talk about passwords—often the least innovative part of the conversation, and yet the one most consistently mishandled. Using the same password across multiple platforms is not just risky—it is reckless. Breach after breach has shown that credential stuffing (using leaked emails and passwords on other services) remains one of the most successful attack methods. Every platform you interact with—whether it's an exchange, forum, or portfolio tracker—must be treated as a potential point of compromise. *Password managers like Bitwarden or 1Password are not optional; they are foundational.*

Two-factor authentication (2FA) must be viewed through a critical lens. SMS-based 2FA—still offered by several major exchanges—should be avoided wherever possible. SIM-swap attacks have devastated even high-profile investors. Instead, hardware keys (YubiKey) or authenticator apps (Aegis, Authy) provide a dramatically improved security posture. But again, the hardware is only as effective as the rigour with which it's used. If your backup codes are stored in your email or in your Google Drive, the advantage is erased.

Then there is the cornerstone of self-custody: the seed phrase. Twelve or twenty-four words that represent your entire wallet—and by extension, your entire net worth in crypto. Writing them down is mandatory. Storing them properly is an art. A seed phrase is *not* safe in a note-taking app, cloud backup, photo album, or password-protected PDF. Air-gapped storage is non-negotiable. This can mean a metal wallet, a paper copy in a secure location, or geographically distributed backups. But more important than the format is your personal *operational secrecy*. Who knows where it is? Who can infer where it might be? Is there any trace of it in your digital life? Every digital breadcrumb increases the chance of exposure.

Some investors complicate this with encryption layers, steganography, or obscure mnemonic tricks. Complexity can be a form of obfuscation—but it also introduces fragility. You must always be able to recover your assets if you're compromised, displaced, or even bereaved. If your digital hygiene is so intricate that it cannot be reassembled without your living memory, it has crossed from defence into dysfunction. *Security must be accessible—not just to you, but to your trusted backup, executor, or legal proxy.*

Next comes your daily behaviour. Do you click links sent in Discord DMs? Do you interact with random airdrops in your wallet? Do you grant smart contract permissions without checking what they allow? These are not hypotheticals—they are day-to-day decisions with real-world consequences. Every web3 site you connect to is asking for access. If you don't check the actual smart contract details, you're essentially signing blank cheques. The crypto community loves the concept of "DYOR"—do your own research—but rarely operationalises it into behaviour. True research is *verification before action.* Not after something breaks.

Digital hygiene also includes *revocation.* Just as you wouldn't leave your house keys with someone you no longer trust, you shouldn't leave smart contract approvals lingering indefinitely. Regularly visit token allowance checkers (such as revoke.cash or Etherscan's approvals page) and strip permissions you no longer need. The principle is simple: *access should expire by default—not remain forever.* Many users have lost assets not from malicious transactions, but from stale approvals granted to now-compromised dApps.

Now let's step back. The point of digital hygiene is not to accumulate more tactics—it is to create an environment where *risky behaviour becomes unlikely.* That environment is psychological as much as it is procedural. It's what Daniel Kahneman might describe as a "System 1 override"—introducing enough friction into fast decisions that you default to caution. Crypto's interface design often pushes toward speed, simplicity, and urgency. But the smart investor installs their own circuit breakers: habits that require reflection, multi-step checks, and redundant confirmations. A high-friction workflow is not inefficient; it is intelligent.

It is worth reflecting on the mindset that digital hygiene demands. Unlike the physical world—where your assets are protected by laws, alarms, and physical custody—the crypto landscape is adversarial by design. Your security assumptions must be inverted: *assume every app wants too much, assume every message could be fake, assume every browser extension is a Trojan horse.* This doesn't mean retreating into paranoia. It means operating with *deliberate posture.*

Even browser hygiene matters more than most realise. Auto-fill? Off. Auto-save passwords? Off. Extensions? Only those you absolutely need. Crypto scams don't require you to type in your private key—they wait for you to install something that logs it for you. The more seamless your browsing experience, the more you may be surrendering without realising it.

And then there's the wider behaviour set—the people you share information with, the forums where you post wallet addresses, the screenshots you share with transaction hashes. Every piece of metadata adds up. Just as burglars scope homes by watching routines, scammers scope victims by watching disclosures. Never assume obscurity is security. *Assume that if it's online, it's indexed. If it's indexed, it's vulnerable.*

Ultimately, digital hygiene is a commitment to *self-respect in the digital age.* It's not about being tech-savvy; it's about being self-aware. The tools are available. The strategies are known. What's lacking, in most cases, is *follow-through.* And follow-through only comes when users reframe security not as something they bolt on after the fact—but as something they *live through* in every interaction.

This is not glamorous. There are no awards for practicing good hygiene. But there is peace of mind. There is resilience. And there is the quiet power of knowing that you are not the low-hanging fruit.

In crypto, you do not get to outsource trust. You *are* the custodian. And your safety is not a setting you toggle—it is a skill you rehearse.

Every. Single. Day.

Your Fear Is Valid—Use It Wisely

Fear is often misunderstood—especially in financial contexts. In boardrooms and brokerage firms alike, it's treated as something to suppress, override, or medicate with spreadsheets. Investors are encouraged to "master their emotions," and phrases like *"be greedy when others are fearful"* are passed off as wisdom. But what if fear—specifically, the alertness it inspires—wasn't the enemy of sound investing, but its quiet ally? What if, particularly in crypto, the presence of fear is not only valid, but essential? In decentralised markets where scams masquerade as startups, and trust is both a marketing slogan and a systemic vulnerability, emotional numbness is not courage—it's exposure.

There is a meaningful difference between panic and vigilance. Panic is reactive, disorienting, and unproductive. Vigilance, on the other hand, is a cultivated posture—one that listens to the cues of discomfort and channels them into strategic caution. Fear that is named, examined, and refined becomes discernment. It becomes pattern recognition. And perhaps most importantly, it becomes habit. In the digital asset space, this kind of internal calibration is more powerful than any external protocol.

Consider how the average crypto scam works: it rarely begins with a brute-force attack on your wallet or an exploit of code. More often, it begins with language. A message. A promise. An air of authority. "You've won a giveaway," or "Urgent action required to secure your funds," or "Click here to join the private presale." These aren't just phishing attempts—they're engineered manipulations of attention and emotion. If you were taught to treat your fear as an error signal rather than an early-warning system, you're more likely to dismiss the tiny spike of unease that might have saved you. Fear doesn't announce itself with sirens; it whispers.

Some of the most cautious people in crypto are also the most experienced—not because they are paranoid, but because they've seen the cost of complacency. They've watched friends drained of their savings by a malicious smart contract. They've heard stories of life savings lost to social engineering. These veterans understand that security is not static. There is no one setting or tool that replaces your responsibility to *notice*. To question. To slow down.

A foundational principle in this space is that *your keys mean your coins*. But a deeper truth might be: *your fear means your focus*. Trustless systems are brilliant in theory, but in practice, the trust gap is filled by human behaviour. This includes your own. If your gut clenches when asked to connect your wallet to a flashy new DApp, pause. That discomfort might not be a sign of ignorance, but of wisdom hard-earned by the collective mistakes of others. Cultivating a relationship with that inner signal—treating it not as a failing but as a feature—creates a psychological perimeter before any technological one.

Let's explore a few examples where fear, used wisely, prevented real harm. In 2022, a crypto investor in Berlin received an unsolicited direct message from what appeared to be a support agent from a well-known DeFi platform. The logo was accurate, the name familiar, and the tone professional. The agent offered to assist with "recent changes to governance protocol," but needed access to the user's seed phrase to proceed. Rather than engage, the investor followed their discomfort, did a quick verification, and discovered it was a copycat profile. No funds were lost—not because of technical security, but because of *emotional intelligence*.

Or consider the cautious ETH holder who declined to mint a "limited-time" NFT drop, despite heavy community pressure and celebrity endorsement. Their reason? The site required wallet permissions far beyond what seemed necessary. Others mocked them for being overly suspicious. A week later, it emerged that the contract contained hidden withdrawal logic. Millions were drained. The cautious investor wasn't lucky—they were attentive. Fear functioned not as paralysis, but as friction—the good kind.

In traditional finance, there are systems of protection: deposit insurance, regulatory enforcement, fraud investigation. But decentralised finance shifts the burden of protection to the individual. That burden can feel overwhelming, particularly to newcomers. Many conflate the discomfort of responsibility with evidence that crypto is "too risky" or "not for them." But what they're really bumping into is the realisation that *autonomy feels dangerous when you haven't learned to listen to yourself.* Crypto does not require recklessness. It requires readiness.

That readiness starts with a reframe: fear is not weakness. It is signal. The real skill lies in learning to decode that signal without letting it devolve into anxiety. Anxiety is speculative—it imagines things going wrong in loops. Fear, by contrast, is situational. It responds to specific signals, and when guided by good information and context, it sharpens your focus. One is paralyzing; the other, catalytic.

But this isn't an argument for becoming hypervigilant or retreating into cynicism. It's an argument for cultivating emotional literacy in parallel with technical skill. Too often, guides on crypto safety skip over the inner work—preferring checklists and devices to habits and intuitions. Yet all the encryption in the world won't protect you if you dismiss your instincts every time something feels off.

Fear, in this context, is also ethical. It prevents overreach. It reminds you that this is real money, not just digital abstraction. It tempers greed, delays impulsivity, and protects you from the intoxication of hype. Without fear, you'll connect your wallet to anything that promises yield. Without fear, you'll delegate decisions to strangers in Discord. Without fear, you'll click the wrong link at the wrong time, and it will be too late.

It's also worth noting that fear scales with exposure. The more assets you accumulate, the more you'll feel the pressure of protecting them. This is not irrational. It's a recognition that risk is cumulative, not isolated. That's why the healthiest investors don't eliminate fear—they *integrate* it. They build systems, routines, and habits that externalise some of that burden. But it begins with a mindset shift: instead of pretending you are fearless, *become fear-literate.*

Ask yourself, when engaging with a platform, connecting a wallet, or responding to a message:
– What's the *source* of this prompt?
– What do they *gain* from my cooperation?
– Is this *urgency* real—or engineered?

These are not just technical questions. They are emotional ones. They require stillness in a culture of speed. They require humility in a culture of overconfidence. And above all, they require that you *respect your discomfort* instead of suppressing it.

Ultimately, safety in crypto is not a set-it-and-forget-it configuration. It's not an app you install or a ledger you hide in a drawer. It is a posture. A process. A way of relating to your environment with attentiveness, not anxiety. Your fear is valid—not because it's always accurate, but because it's yours. When paired with good information and self-respect, it becomes your most valuable tool in a market that respects no one unless they respect themselves first.

Chapter 7
Cold Wallets and the Art of Disconnection

There is a discipline—quiet, unfashionable, but vital—that distinguishes the casual speculator from the deliberate steward of digital wealth: the practice of disconnection. In an age where the pulse of markets is beamed endlessly into pockets and minds, to choose absence from the network appears almost perverse. Yet cold storage, that act of tucking assets offline, is not a retreat into obscurity but a calculated refusal of distraction. It is a refusal to live at the mercy of notifications. Cold storage is not only about security; it is about sovereignty of attention. It is a declaration that urgency does not dictate importance.

To grasp the meaning of cold wallets, one must first reckon with the psychic atmosphere of crypto itself. It is not just volatile in value; it is volatile in rhythm. Constant launches, governance votes, liquidity cycles, airdrop rumours—it creates a relentless demand to "be there." Hot wallets, browser plug-ins, mobile trading apps: they promise immediacy but extract vigilance. One becomes a watchman over one's holdings, always on call, knowing that one false move could cost everything. Against this backdrop, cold storage is less a bunker and more a sanctuary. It is not silence as avoidance, but silence as strength.

But what does going offline really entail? Not a weekend detox or a token gesture, but a structural choice. To take wealth that demands constant attention and place it in a form that insists on patience. Hardware devices like Ledger or Trezor, yes—but also paper wallets, multisig schemes, or air-gapped machines. These are not just tools of convenience. They are philosophical instruments. They say: I trust my convictions enough to remove them from reach.

Yet here lies a common mistake. Too many treat cold storage as a box to be ticked. Buy a device, follow a tutorial, announce "done." But the work has hardly begun. What deserves cold treatment? Why? For how long? And how will retrieval happen, when it must? A hardware wallet is not a solution; it is a starting point. The teenager buying memecoins does not need the same architecture as the DAO treasury managing millions. Cold storage is not a standardised script. It is an alignment exercise.

Some assets demand mobility—staked tokens that require governance activity, yield-bearing positions, NFTs tied into protocols. Others thrive in stillness: Bitcoin intended for decades, stablecoins as emergency reserves, blue-chip assets as bedrock. Cold storage asks for discernment. To lock up everything is not prudence—it is rigidity. To lock away what is essential, and let the rest remain agile, is the art.

And then, the other half of the equation: retrieval. Many lock up wealth only to stumble when faced with re-access. The irony is sharp—protection turning into obstruction. The wisest cold storage designs are not about absence but about intentional re-entry. They ask: when you come back, in what conditions will you do so? On what machine, with which rituals, under what safeguards? The act of retrieval becomes almost ceremonial. Not casual, not rushed, but undertaken with clarity.

Another illusion worth dismantling: that hardware is everything. It isn't. A ledger device may be built like a fortress, but if your seed phrase is photographed and uploaded to the cloud, the fortress door stands wide open. If you tape an envelope marked "wallet backup" under your desk, your cleverness is undone. Hardware is necessary, but insufficient. The real battleground is habit. Cold storage is, at heart, a behavioural discipline masquerading as a technological solution.

Equally, it should not be a reflex to panic. Too many rush into cold setups after a hack, a market dip, a sensational headline. Reaction breeds poor architecture. Cold storage ought to be deliberate—an integrated element of your investment design. It forces hard questions: What liquidity do you require? How quickly? Who must have access if you are gone? They are uncomfortable, but unavoidable. In truth, cold storage is not so different from estate planning. It requires confrontation with permanence.

Cold storage also restores something crypto culture desperately undervalues: friction. Everywhere, the language of haste dominates—"ape in," "buy the dip," "farm the yield." Cold storage interrupts. It requires pause, ceremony even. That pause is not inefficiency; it is protection. Friction acts as a sieve, filtering out the urge to act on impulse. And in a world where one impulsive confirmation can erase years of care, friction is a blessing.

Beneath the mechanics lies the emotional core. Cold storage is not avoided because it is technically difficult; it is avoided because it is emotionally demanding. It requires choices. It requires facing one's mortality, one's priorities, one's sense of permanence. To place assets in cold storage is to admit you are planning for more than the next chart. It is, in many ways, the most adult act in crypto.

Which leads to a paradox. The most sophisticated investors are often the quietest. They are not glued to price feeds or broadcasting every move. Their wealth is not loudly visible but carefully placed beyond reach. They are serene not because they are indifferent, but because they have already decided. They chose design over distraction, calm over compulsion.

By the time this chapter closes, the reader will know more than how to configure a cold wallet. They will understand why it matters—and how the very act of disconnecting reshapes one's relationship with wealth. Cold storage is not exile. It is authorship. Disconnection, when chosen wisely, is not absence at all. It is sovereignty.

In Praise of Going Offline

The phrase "not your keys, not your coins" is often repeated like a mantra in the world of digital assets, but its depth is rarely lived. In a space obsessed with speed, liquidity, and always-on interfaces, the concept of deliberate disconnection is almost countercultural. Yet for the serious investor—one who isn't here for noise but for meaning—there comes a moment when leaving the internet behind is not just an act of technical security, but of personal clarity. Cold storage, at its essence, is not a tool—it's a philosophy. *It reclaims silence from signal, and sovereignty from servers.*

To grasp what cold storage truly represents, one must look beyond hardware. Ledger and Trezor may be brand names, but they are also artefacts of a deeper intention: the commitment to step away from the chaos and protect something in a place where no algorithm can reach it. This is not paranoia. It is presence. The decision to move assets offline is not a retreat from innovation—it is the mature embrace of responsibility. In a system where trust is not delegated but earned, cold storage is the closest one can come to financial solitude.

The risk of being perpetually online is not only technical. Certainly, hot wallets and browser-based access leave you vulnerable to malware, phishing, and exploits. But there is a subtler erosion that happens too: the erosion of discernment. Constant exposure to price charts, hype cycles, and social influence keeps your assets in emotional motion, not just digital availability. A wallet connected to the internet is also connected to your reflexes. *Cold storage severs that wire. It reintroduces latency, not as a bug, but as a feature of sanity.*

Consider the psychological architecture of a cold wallet. Unlike the UI-driven immediacy of an app, these tools require intention. You must plug in a device, confirm an address, verify on a second screen, perhaps even enter a passphrase you haven't used in months. Every step reasserts that your assets are *yours*—and that they will not move without your hand. The very friction that some find annoying is what restores gravity to your decisions. When money is this inert, it becomes harder to treat like adrenaline.

This is precisely why so few embrace it. Cold storage doesn't flatter our need to check, tweak, and tinker. There's nothing addictive about it. It doesn't push notifications or show trending tokens. It has no feed. And that's the point. *A secure investor is often a bored one.* The digital economy thrives on engagement; your attention is a monetisable asset. Cold wallets flip the dynamic: they reward disengagement. They protect not just your coins, but your cognition.

To illustrate the contrast, examine two real-world investor profiles. One keeps their funds in a popular mobile wallet, constantly updated with market news, and has made a dozen trades this month based on Twitter sentiment. The other moved the majority of their holdings to a hardware wallet three years ago, has no active alerts, and spends their time reading whitepapers instead of watching candlesticks. Who will likely experience greater long-term resilience? Who is less likely to panic sell in a flash crash or fall for a too-good-to-be-true airdrop scam? *Security is behavioural before it is technical.*

Of course, cold storage is not without its challenges. It introduces a different kind of vulnerability: operational diligence. If you lose your seed phrase or fail to create a secure backup strategy, there is no customer support to call. But here again, there is a deeper lesson. Cold storage teaches you that *your competence matters*. There is no outsourcing of care. And in a world increasingly engineered to reduce user friction, that is both rare and powerful. You are not merely saving assets; you are cultivating vigilance.

The cultural implications are worth unpacking. The architecture of crypto may be decentralised, but much of its day-to-day usage is not. Wallets connected to exchanges, apps that rely on APIs, yield farming protocols with auto-compound features—these are all functionally dependent on constant connection. The myth of sovereignty is often just that: a myth. Cold storage slices through the rhetoric. It asks the simplest question: *Could you still access your wealth if the internet disappeared for a week?* If the answer is no, you don't own it. You're renting confidence from a third party.

There's also a philosophical symmetry to consider. Bitcoin, by design, is a slow settlement system. Ethereum's evolution to proof-of-stake retains complexity but rewards patience. These are not technologies optimised for instant gratification—they are infrastructures for long-term value. Cold storage harmonises with this ethic. It extends the rhythm of the base layer into your personal habits. *Your method of storage should mirror your investment thesis.* If you believe in the long arc of decentralised value, then holding your keys offline is not just safer—it is truer.

And yet, this act is deeply human. Behind the encryption, the cryptography, and the seed phrases is a person making a choice: to trust themselves. That is the real threshold. Many avoid cold storage not because it is difficult, but because it removes the illusion of protection. When you are the last line of defence, there is no one left to blame. This is not a failure—it is maturity. It's what separates holders from speculators, and stewards from consumers.

Even the ritual of accessing a cold wallet can be reimagined as a moment of awareness. Think of it less as a tech operation and more like opening a vault. When you retrieve assets from cold storage, you are not just moving funds—you are reaffirming intent. That kind of slowness is rare in finance. It creates space for reflection. It reminds you that not everything should be immediate, and not every signal is urgent. *In a system built for speed, disconnection becomes a radical act.*

The future of self-custody may evolve with newer devices, air-gapped tools, or even biometric failsafes. But the foundational posture remains the same: step back, take control, and value stillness. Cold storage is not about being anti-technology. It is about choosing *which* technologies to trust—and on *whose* terms. It's the difference between owning your house and leasing a condo in a high-rise with 24/7 surveillance.

Ultimately, cold storage is less a practice than a posture. It is the digital expression of what ancient wisdom has always known: that stillness is power, and that what you protect with intention stays protected. Whether you're safeguarding a few hundred pounds or a life-changing fortune, going offline is not a withdrawal—it's a deepening. It is a return to agency, a recalibration of values, and a quiet rebellion against the tyranny of connectivity. *In cold storage, peace is not a metaphor. It is a protocol.*

Choosing the Right Cold Storage Method

Security, like identity, is context-dependent. It cannot be universalised without compromise, and nowhere is this clearer than in the realm of cold storage. The decision to go offline with your digital assets is not a mere operational step—it is a declaration of values. But once that decision is made, a more nuanced set of questions follows. *Who are you? What exactly are you securing? And against what threat model?* The cold storage method you choose should not reflect hype or brand loyalty, but alignment with your specific needs, risks, and temperament.

For the cautious professional managing moderate long-term holdings, a single hardware wallet may offer elegant sufficiency. For an organisation stewarding multi-million-pound treasuries, a multisignature architecture might be non-negotiable. And for the radically minimal or deeply private, even a paper wallet—though misunderstood and often maligned—can serve as an intentional act of sovereignty. The sophistication of your storage method should match the complexity of your life, not the volume of your coins.

Let us begin with the hardware wallets that dominate most conversations: Ledger and Trezor. These devices are purpose-built for secure offline key management. They do not merely store private keys—they isolate them. When properly used, they prevent the key from ever touching an internet-connected device. But their security is not automatic. They require users to understand what they are doing, to verify addresses on the device screen itself, to avoid blind signing, and to rigorously protect recovery phrases. *A tool is only as good as its operator, and this is doubly true when the tool involves cryptography.*

Ledger has earned both acclaim and criticism for its sleek design, wide compatibility, and growing app ecosystem. It's the Apple of hardware wallets—user-friendly, highly integrated, but proprietary in certain ways that provoke discomfort in purists. A notable controversy in 2023 arose around its "Ledger Recover" feature, which—though opt-in—proposed encrypted backups of seed phrases with third-party custodians. This triggered a deep philosophical debate: *Should a cold wallet ever even offer that possibility?* It reminded users that convenience is often the front door through which risk walks in.

Trezor, in contrast, has maintained a stricter open-source posture. It appeals to users who prioritise auditability over polish. Trezor devices may feel less modern but more ideologically aligned with crypto's cypherpunk ethos. Their transparency, however, puts more onus on the user to manage firmware and updates wisely. In the wrong hands, openness can become a vector of vulnerability rather than a pillar of trust.

Still, hardware wallets are not immune to supply chain risk. A compromised device received from an unverified source can quietly leak secrets before you even power it on. This is why experts consistently advise purchasing directly from manufacturers, avoiding resellers entirely. And while the risk of physical tampering may seem remote to casual users, *cold storage is for serious stakes—it is precisely the long tail of rare but catastrophic events that one aims to defend against.*

Beyond devices, there is the realm of paper wallets—simple printouts or handwritten representations of a private key or seed phrase. Dismissed by many as outdated or insecure, they remain relevant when wielded wisely. Their security lies not in cryptographic strength but in physical obscurity. A paper wallet stored in a fireproof safe, with no digital trace, is a fortress by omission. But they are brittle: a coffee spill, a house fire, or an accidental discard can erase wealth in seconds. Unlike hardware wallets, they lack built-in safeguards against human error. *The paper wallet does not forgive.*

Then there is the emerging domain of multisignature storage. This involves dividing custody among multiple devices, locations, or people. No single key can access the assets. A typical scheme might require 2-of-3 or 3-of-5 signatures to authorise a transaction. This architecture is conceptually elegant—it replaces trust in any one actor with a distributed quorum model. It also introduces complexity: key management, redundancy, and recovery planning become engineering problems in themselves. Tools like Casa, Unchained, and Electrum offer multisig support, but using them correctly requires fluency in wallet software, secure backups, and often coordination with other participants.

Multisig shines in organisational settings, family trusts, or when significant generational wealth is at stake. It allows a founder, for example, to remain one key among several—removing the risk of single-point compromise. But for the average retail investor, multisig may feel like overkill. Simplicity is a security model too. *If you cannot explain your system to your future self, you do not have a system—you have a liability.*

This brings us to the heart of the matter: choosing the right cold storage method is not a technical problem, it is a clarity problem. Begin not with the wallet, but with an honest profile of your holdings, risk appetite, digital fluency, and emotional discipline. Are your assets meant for inheritance, active management, or emergency funds? Will you need access quarterly, annually, or only if disaster strikes? Is there someone else who should be able to retrieve them if you are incapacitated? These questions map your context—and context is the only sensible compass in cold storage design.

The worst cold storage method is not the least sophisticated—it is the one you abandon out of confusion or never test under real-world conditions. Far too many users have purchased hardware wallets, set them up once, and then ignored them for years—only to discover later that they misplaced their seed phrase, forgot the pin, or failed to update firmware now incompatible with modern wallet software. *Cold storage is not a one-time event. It is a living relationship with your assets.*

Moreover, consider the role of redundancy. A single device stored in one location is a fragile point of failure. If the house burns down, or if the device is lost during a move, recovery depends entirely on whether your backups were accurate, secure, and accessible. Redundancy, however, must be strategic. Simply making more copies increases exposure. The goal is not duplication, but resilience. One solution is to store shards of your seed phrase in separate locations—or even to use mnemonic splitting tools like Shamir's Secret Sharing, which divides the phrase into recoverable subsets. These methods are not intuitive. But when studied carefully, they offer powerful defence without undue exposure.

Finally, any storage method—hardware, paper, or multisig—must be documented for your future self or designated heirs. This is often the most overlooked aspect of cold storage. Without thoughtful documentation, even perfect security becomes a prison. *An inaccessible wallet is indistinguishable from theft.* This is where cold storage intersects with estate planning, legal clarity, and familial trust. Cold wallets do not die, but their owners do. Plan accordingly.

In selecting a method, then, do not ask, "What is the best cold wallet?" Ask, "What is the wisest way to hold what matters most to me, with the least reliance on memory, luck, or heroics?" That question reframes security as not just an act of protection—but of personal maturity.

Storing What Matters, Forgetting What Doesn't

In an age where digital hoarding is increasingly normalised, the wisdom of discernment has become a rare but invaluable skill. Nowhere is this more evident than in crypto asset management. The instinct to secure everything—to treat every token, every dust-level airdrop, every novelty coin as precious—has quietly become a liability disguised as diligence. What if the smarter move isn't to secure everything, but to secure what truly matters and let go of the rest?

Cold storage is not a default vault for everything you own in crypto. It is a deliberate filter. When you move an asset offline, you're not just protecting it—you're declaring its relevance to your long-term financial vision. To store something in cold storage is to make a statement: *this will still matter to me in a decade.* That level of clarity requires more than just technical understanding; it demands philosophical restraint.

The allure of perfect protection has become a trap of its own. Beginners often assume that the endpoint of crypto security is simply cold storage, as if tucking everything into a Ledger or Trezor will solve all problems. But throwing your entire digital portfolio into a vault without first conducting strategic triage is like packing every object in your house into a bomb shelter: you may be safe, but you'll be surrounded by irrelevance, clutter, and confusion. *Security without selectivity is just elaborate hoarding.*

The first task, then, is not how to store, but *what to store.* And answering that requires a confrontation with value—real, enduring value—not temporary price action or speculative hype. Ask: does this asset represent a long-term thesis? Does it have economic or utility weight that will persist across market cycles? If it disappeared from your portfolio, would your financial architecture be compromised—or would it simply sting your ego?

Consider the anatomy of a typical crypto portfolio: a mix of core positions (e.g., Bitcoin, Ethereum), experimental plays (e.g., Layer 2s, niche DeFi protocols), legacy tokens from old projects, and a scattering of airdrops, memecoins, or illiquid tokens that seemed interesting at the time. Now imagine trying to manage all of that in cold storage. Do you create multiple wallets? Duplicate seed phrases? Catalogue everything in spreadsheets? At some point, the friction becomes the flaw.

The logic of minimalism begins to assert itself. Bitcoin held for the long term, or Ethereum staked but not actively traded, may clearly deserve cold storage. But your LP tokens in a yield farming protocol? Your highly volatile speculative tokens that you might flip next month? These are not cold storage candidates—they're *liquidity instruments*, not *store-of-value instruments*. Cold storage should reflect permanence, not preference.

Even within so-called core holdings, nuance matters. For example, if you own Ethereum in multiple contexts—some for staking, some for governance, some as collateral—do all of those holdings belong in the same offline vault? Not necessarily. A multisig wallet for governance votes might serve one purpose, while long-term ETH allocated for generational wealth might deserve air-gapped cold storage. The method should reflect the meaning.

Security experts often emphasise reducing attack surfaces. But this principle applies to cognitive bandwidth as well. Every asset you store demands memory, attention, and ritual. Seed phrases must be remembered or physically stored. Wallets must be labelled and monitored. Retrieval processes must be documented. If you decentralise your assets across too many vaults, you don't just fragment your storage—you fragment your sanity.

To clarify what matters, invert the question: what would you *not* regret losing? If you're honest, you'll discover that much of your portfolio exists out of curiosity, inertia, or optimism—not conviction. Cold storage should be reserved for assets with conviction. That's not just good security; it's good psychology.

The practice of triage also prevents another, subtler risk: over-engineering. Cold storage setups can become comically complex in the pursuit of absolute safety—metal seed plates, geographically distributed recovery shards, time-locked multisig smart contracts.

These may be justifiable for institutional-grade holdings, but for an individual investor with under six figures in core assets, this can be disproportionate. Complexity itself becomes an attack vector—*the enemy is often not the hacker, but your future self forgetting what you did.*

What you forget becomes critical. If you store a token in cold storage and forget the wallet it lives in, or worse, the asset itself, you've essentially self-rugged. Forgotten assets are as inaccessible as stolen ones. There's a growing digital graveyard of crypto wealth—not lost through hacks, but through forgetfulness. This is the psychological cost of over-retention.

There is also a trust economy at play. If your storage setup requires coordination with multiple parties—co-signers, trusted family members, legal custodians—you must ask not only what you're storing, but who must remember it, honour it, and execute it. Cold storage is often framed as an individual act of sovereignty. But in reality, long-term storage is a *relational* act—it's a bet that your future self or your heirs will understand what you meant to protect.

Consider the lessons from estate planning. The most common cause of unclaimed inheritances in crypto is not technological failure, but unclear intent. Loved ones are left with seed phrases they don't recognise, or wallets they can't connect to anything meaningful. Simplicity isn't just convenience; *it is an act of compassion* toward those who may one day inherit the complexity you've built.

None of this is an argument against cold storage—it is an argument for disciplined cold storage. The discipline is twofold: store only what matters, and make sure that what matters can be recovered. The rest—dust, hype, expired bets—should be allowed to fade. If an asset is not worth the burden of protection, it is not worth protecting.

This is not an easy mindset. It resists the ego's urge to catalogue everything, to never miss out, to preserve every decision in case it proves to be genius in hindsight. But crypto rewards clarity over clutter. *The fewer assets you have to think about, the more you can think clearly.*

As the ecosystem matures, so too must the investor. The early years of crypto were marked by an accumulation impulse—more tokens, more wallets, more tools, more risk. The coming era will be defined by strategic subtraction. Cold storage is not about building a digital fortress. It is about curating a vault of personal meaning.

The art, then, is in the cut. The investor who masters storage is not the one with the most complex system or the most diversified vault. It is the one who can say, with unshakable clarity: *this is what matters*. Everything else can be safely forgotten.

Rituals of Retrieval

For most investors, accessing funds is an instinctual act—fluid, frequent, and frictionless. A few taps on a screen, a fingerprint, and capital moves. But cold storage changes the rhythm. When assets are kept offline, retrieval is not casual; it is deliberate. This delay, often seen as a technical inconvenience, is in fact its core philosophical strength. *The friction forces reflection.* Retrieval becomes a ritual, not a reflex. And that shift is profound.

The conventional view of crypto management centres on speed: instant access, instant swaps, instant liquidity. But this mindset, borrowed from traditional finance and turbocharged by the user interfaces of centralised exchanges, presumes that immediacy is inherently good. It isn't. In fact, the lack of delay often feeds the worst investor behaviours—panic selling, impulse buying, overtrading, or reacting to market noise. Cold storage, by contrast, introduces time as a safeguard. You cannot impulsively trade what you must consciously retrieve.

This delay builds a useful buffer between emotion and action. It allows the investor to move from reactive to reflective. And reflection is where real strategy lives. By forcing a pause, cold storage invites a different question—not "what is the market doing?" but *"why am I touching this asset at all?"*

Each retrieval, then, is an interrogation: Has the reason I stored this changed? Has my personal context shifted? Is this a reaction or a realignment?

When retrieval is made difficult enough to require thought—but not so difficult as to discourage execution—you create the optimal conditions for intention. The process of reconnecting to your long-term vault becomes a kind of ritual. Not mystical, but procedural—precise steps, confirmed identities, redundant checks. In this structure, trust is not blind—it is engineered.

It's worth recognising that most financial systems train us to act quickly and trust systems implicitly. Credit card transactions clear instantly. Bank transfers settle in hours. Password resets take seconds. But crypto custody—especially cold custody—demands that we turn this conditioning on its head. Retrieval requires not only time but *trust in our past self*: in how well we prepared, documented, and protected access.

This retrospective trust introduces a uniquely human vulnerability. What if I've forgotten the PIN? What if the recovery phrase is incomplete? What if the instructions are ambiguous? Retrieval tests not just your setup but your foresight. Cold storage is not a set-it-and-forget-it solution—it is a long-term relationship with your own memory.

Some seasoned users formalise this process. They create retrieval rituals not only for security but for clarity. One investor, for example, sets quarterly calendar events titled "Asset Reconnection", during which they review their cold wallets—not to move anything, but simply to verify their readiness. Others write down a full walkthrough of retrieval steps and store it in a sealed envelope, updated annually, as part of their estate planning protocol. These rituals serve two purposes: operational continuity and psychological assurance. *The very act of periodic verification reinforces sovereignty.*

Ritualising retrieval also deepens the symbolic gravity of what is stored. It says: these assets are not just numbers on a ledger. They are representations of strategy, conviction, future. Retrieval is therefore not just technical—it's a reaffirmation of belief.

The contrast with hot wallets is instructive. In a hot wallet, assets feel always at hand. This creates a subtle illusion: that they are perpetually usable, even disposable. The cognitive distance between possession and action is thin. But in cold storage, retrieval becomes its own event. You must set aside time, prepare tools, often enter a specific location or open a secure envelope. It mimics a kind of ceremony: intention, action, result. And like all good ceremonies, it is remembered.

There's also an important social dimension. In many cold storage configurations—particularly multisig or legally shared setups—retrieval is not solitary. It requires communication, cooperation, consensus. You must reach out to other signatories. You must explain, justify, perhaps even persuade. In doing so, you introduce social friction—but also social accountability. This is where disconnection becomes not a weakness, but a governance strength. *Cold storage forces conversation.*

This can be especially powerful in institutional or family settings. A multi-generational cold wallet, for instance, creates structured touchpoints across time. Retrieval becomes a moment of instruction, or even initiation: a teaching opportunity for the next custodian. You're not just handing them access; you're transferring context.

And context is everything. A retrieval process without context is a liability. The heir who inherits a hardware wallet but not the reasons for its contents is at a loss. The executor who holds a multisig key but not the playbook risks freezing value indefinitely. Retrieval rituals must encode not only process, but purpose.

That's why documentation is not optional. It is the silent partner in every retrieval ritual. The investor who treats notes, guides, and off-chain instructions as part of the system—not ancillary to it—builds a vault that is not only secure, but *translatable.* After all, the ultimate goal of cold storage is not permanence of protection, but *continuity of access across time and people.*

Still, rituals require maintenance. They must be rehearsed, not just designed. A retrieval process that was clear two years ago may be murky now. Tools get outdated. Hardware devices degrade. People forget. The point of ritual is not perfection—it's to create a reliable minimum standard under imperfect conditions. You should be able to recover funds even if you're under stress, abroad, or acting on someone else's behalf. That is not redundancy—it is responsibility.

And this responsibility is ethical as much as technical. If you've chosen disconnection as your safety model, you've also chosen to make trust a deliberate act. Not trust in systems, but in structure. Not in automation, but in preparation. Retrieval becomes the test of your commitment to that structure. *A failed retrieval is not a failed system; it's a failed intention.*

Yet perhaps the deepest insight is this: retrieval is not always a technical act. Sometimes it is emotional. To access a vault is to look backwards—to remember the mindset in which something was stored. Were you bullish, cautious, idealistic? What did you believe then that you may doubt now? Retrieval surfaces not just assets, but assumptions. This can be uncomfortable. But it is also clarifying. *The act of retrieval is a confrontation with your own thinking over time.*

In this light, the real purpose of retrieval rituals becomes clearer. It is not only about accessing capital. It is about preserving clarity. About maintaining a thread between who you were and who you are. About ensuring that value—real, intentional value—is never abandoned to time, forgetfulness, or fear.

If cold storage is about protection, then retrieval is about precision. Not just in mechanics, but in meaning. And when practiced with care, that precision can be transformative. It turns disconnection into design. Security into stewardship. Access into alignment.

That is the art of the retrieval ritual. Not just knowing how to recover, but knowing *why you stored something in the first place—and whether it still deserves your trust.*

Chapter 8
Strategy Over Speculation

In the clamorous arena of digital assets—where headlines trumpet overnight millionaires and charts strobe with dizzying velocity—the virtue of restraint can appear almost counterintuitive. Yet it is precisely here, amidst the clamour, that stillness proves its worth. This chapter opens with a provocation: perhaps the most decisive action an investor can take is, paradoxically, inaction. To resist the twitch of the finger on the trade button, to sit through the storm without flinching, is not laziness. It is composure. It is strategy. In a culture intoxicated with immediacy, the discipline to wait is a rare weapon indeed.

From this foundation, the discussion shifts to dollar-cost averaging—not as some sterile arithmetic trick, but as something closer to a ritual. To commit funds at regular intervals is, in one sense, banal; in another, it is an act of emotional discipline. DCA tempers the ego's hunger to outwit markets, to pounce on dips or flee at spikes. It demands humility, patience, and an acceptance that time, not timing, does the heavy lifting. What might seem mechanical becomes almost meditative—a steady rhythm against the chaos.

This naturally widens into the question of horizons. How long, exactly, is the true investor willing to wait? The chapter invites a radical shift of imagination: from days and weeks to years and decades. Such a recalibration unsettles, for it runs against the grain of a culture hooked on speed. Yet to think long is to trade adrenaline for endurance. Patience, here, is recast as the most precious of crypto's assets—rarer than any token, more enduring than any yield. Case studies, models, and history all point to the same conclusion: durable conviction outlasts frenetic reaction.

And then, portfolio construction—often reduced to allocation charts and percentage breakdowns—is reimagined in more intimate terms. An investment portfolio is, in truth, a kind of autobiography. It should mirror not merely the logic of markets but the texture of a life: one's age, obligations, ambitions, and values. To invest without this self-knowledge is to borrow someone else's map. This chapter urges clarity, almost ruthlessness, in aligning capital with identity.

Taken together, these threads weave a vision of investing that resists spectacle. It is intellectual, yes, but not detached; practical, but never mechanical. It asks the reader to move past speculation into something sturdier, slower, and infinitely more personal. Amidst the roar of markets and the siren songs of haste, the chapter points towards a quieter strength: the deliberate art of restraint. Here lies not the absence of action, but its most refined form.

The Discipline of Not Acting-

In a market defined by volatility, rapid innovation, and constant noise, the instinct to act—to buy, sell, or reposition oneself at every perceived opportunity—can seem almost reflexive. Yet, it is precisely within this tumultuous environment that *not* acting becomes a formidable discipline. The discipline of not acting is counterintuitive; it requires mastering patience, resisting impulse, and cultivating a deliberate stillness amid the chaos. This restraint is not a passive surrender but an active, conscious choice—a strategic posture that distinguishes the prudent investor from the restless speculator. Understanding when to wait, and how to wait with intention, transforms the seemingly inactive into the profoundly powerful.

Central to this practice is recognising that markets, particularly those surrounding digital assets, are subject to cycles of hype, fear, and irrational exuberance. The temptation to respond swiftly to breaking news, price swings, or social media fervour can lead to costly mistakes. Consider the archetypal tale of the investor who buys near a peak out of fear of missing out, only to panic sell during the inevitable downturn. This pattern, repeated countless times, underscores the perils of reactive behaviour. The discipline of not acting demands the cultivation of a mindset that sees beyond immediate fluctuations and embraces a longer temporal horizon. This perspective reframes market movements as *noise* rather than *signals*—inviting the investor to listen carefully, yet choose their moment to engage judiciously.

One profound example of this principle can be found in the strategy of "strategic patience" employed by some of the most successful investors across history. Legendary figures like Warren Buffett have emphasised the value of waiting for the right opportunity rather than chasing every market trend. Buffett's approach of "waiting for the fat pitch" exemplifies the discipline of not acting impulsively but positioning oneself to capitalise on moments of genuine value. While the context of crypto markets differs in many respects, the underlying wisdom remains relevant: deliberate patience is a skill, not a default state of inaction.

But how does one cultivate such discipline amid the unrelenting barrage of information and emotional triggers? The answer lies in developing *intentional waiting*—an active engagement with time rather than its passive surrender. Intentional waiting involves setting clear criteria for action based on personal investment theses, risk tolerance, and long-term goals. It means defining beforehand what conditions would justify entering or exiting a position and then steadfastly adhering to these principles despite external pressures. This disciplined waiting fosters emotional regulation, reducing the likelihood of decisions driven by fear, greed, or social contagion.

Moreover, intentional waiting is undergirded by a nuanced understanding of market psychology. Markets are not purely rational arenas; they are human ecosystems marked by collective behaviours, biases, and cognitive errors. Recognising these dynamics allows the investor to anticipate phases of overreaction or complacency and position themselves accordingly. It shifts the investor's role from that of a frantic responder to a thoughtful observer and measured participant. This transformation is essential for navigating the unique complexities of crypto markets, where speculative excesses are amplified and volatility is often extreme.

The discipline of not acting also challenges the common misconception that successful investing requires constant monitoring and frequent transactions. On the contrary, empirical research consistently shows that excessive trading erodes returns through transaction costs, tax implications, and behavioural pitfalls. In the crypto space, where fees can be high and tax regulations evolving, the costs of overactivity are particularly salient. Thus, adopting a measured pace—where actions are sparing but well-considered—becomes a strategic imperative.

Furthermore, embracing the discipline of not acting does not imply disengagement from ongoing learning or portfolio review. It encourages a rhythm of thoughtful reflection, re-evaluation, and readiness to act *when* conditions genuinely warrant. This balance between vigilance and patience is delicate but achievable. Tools such as automated alerts, periodic portfolio reviews, and clearly articulated investment frameworks support the investor in maintaining this equilibrium.

The challenge, of course, is emotional. Humans are wired for action; waiting can feel uncomfortable or even counterproductive. Here, cultivating *meta-awareness*—the ability to observe one's own impulses without immediately yielding to them—is vital. Practices drawn from mindfulness and behavioural psychology can aid investors in recognising the physiological and psychological cues that prompt premature action. By learning to sit with discomfort and uncertainty, the investor strengthens their capacity for disciplined waiting.

Real-world examples from crypto investors illustrate both the triumphs and trials of this discipline. Stories abound of individuals who resisted the siren call of panic selling during downturns, maintaining conviction and ultimately realising significant gains. Conversely, narratives of those who chased every spike or succumbed to herd behaviour serve as cautionary tales. These lived experiences reinforce that the discipline of not acting is less about the absence of activity and more about the presence of wisdom.

Ultimately, this chapter invites readers to reconceptualise inactivity not as hesitation or indecision but as a purposeful strategy—a form of patience that is both rare and potent. The discipline of not acting, when embraced with intention and clarity, becomes a foundation upon which sustainable, resilient investing is built. It is an invitation to rise above the market noise, to respect the passage of time, and to trust that sometimes the most profound power lies in waiting well.

By learning when—and how—to wait, the reader gains a toolkit not only for crypto investing but for approaching uncertainty in life more broadly. This mastery over impulsivity fosters not just financial steadiness but a deeper sense of agency and calm. In a world that rewards haste, the discipline of not acting offers a radical alternative: thoughtful stillness as a pathway to lasting success.

Dollar-Cost Averaging as a Spiritual Practice-

In the fast-paced, often frenetic world of cryptocurrency investing, the allure of rapid gains can obscure the profound value of restraint and rhythm. Dollar-cost averaging (DCA), frequently dismissed as a mere mechanical strategy, warrants a deeper re-examination—not solely as a financial technique but as a discipline imbued with emotional regulation and respect for time. Far from being a passive or simplistic approach, DCA invites investors into a sustained, mindful engagement with their assets, transforming the act of investing into a form of deliberate practice that honours patience and steadiness amidst volatility.

At its core, dollar-cost averaging involves systematically investing a fixed amount at regular intervals, irrespective of market conditions. This strategy inherently counters the human tendency to time the market—a tendency that, despite centuries of investment history, remains stubbornly elusive for most. However, beyond the surface mechanics lies a more nuanced dimension: DCA functions as a stabilising force for the investor's psyche, providing a disciplined framework through which emotional impulses are tempered. In markets known for extreme swings and noise, this emotional steadiness becomes as valuable as any technical advantage.

The psychological benefits of DCA are well-documented. By committing to invest consistently over time, individuals mitigate the anxiety and regret that often accompany attempts at market timing. Each incremental investment becomes a ritual that fosters a sense of control and purpose. This ritualistic quality echoes practices found in contemplative traditions, where regular, intentional actions cultivate mindfulness and resilience. Viewed through this lens, DCA is not merely about accumulating assets but about cultivating an attitude—one that embraces uncertainty with calm resolve and honours the unfolding of value over extended horizons.

Historical examples abound where investors who adhered to disciplined DCA strategies outperformed their more reactive peers. For instance, during the crypto market cycles of the past decade, many seasoned participants who maintained consistent entry points over years weathered severe downturns with composure, ultimately benefiting from cumulative gains. Conversely, those who chased fads or succumbed to panic often faced disproportionate losses. The discipline to act consistently, irrespective of short-term noise, is what differentiated success from failure—a testament to DCA's efficacy as both a practical and psychological tool.

Beyond individual anecdotes, the notion of time-honouring embedded in DCA resonates with broader economic and philosophical insights. Time preference—the value individuals assign to present versus future consumption—shapes financial decision-making profoundly. Crypto markets, characterised by rapid innovation and speculative excess, challenge investors to recalibrate their time preference toward patience. DCA embodies this recalibration, encouraging a future-oriented mindset that balances hope with prudence. This shift is not trivial; it realigns investing from a game of chance to a considered commitment, where wealth creation is tethered to enduring belief rather than fleeting trends.

Moreover, DCA's spiritual dimension emerges in its capacity to transform volatility from a source of distress into a mechanism for opportunity. By investing steadily, one naturally buys more during price dips and less when prices rise, smoothing entry points and reducing regret. This pattern exemplifies a harmony with market rhythms rather than resistance to them. The investor becomes attuned not only to financial cycles but to their own internal rhythms—developing a form of self-mastery that transcends mere market participation.

However, embracing DCA as a spiritual practice demands more than rote execution; it requires conscious engagement and intentionality. This involves setting clear investment goals aligned with one's values, defining a sustainable contribution schedule, and committing to the process despite inevitable external pressures. Importantly, this approach invites reflection on one's relationship to money, risk, and time—questions often sidelined in the pursuit of quick profits. Such reflection enriches the investing journey, embedding it within a broader life narrative marked by discipline, humility, and foresight.

Challenges to this approach are not insignificant. Critics may argue that rigid adherence to DCA ignores market conditions and may lead to missed opportunities during sustained bull markets. While market awareness remains important, the core value of DCA lies in its emotional and temporal discipline rather than predictive precision. The capacity to maintain equanimity during downturns and resist impulsive shifts is often the determinant of long-term success. In this respect, DCA provides a behavioural anchor amid market turbulence.

Contemporary tools and platforms further facilitate the disciplined practice of DCA, automating contributions and reinforcing consistency. Yet technology alone cannot replace the intentional mindset crucial to its success. Investors must cultivate patience and emotional intelligence, recognising that the true returns of DCA unfold not only in portfolio balances but in the development of enduring virtues.

Ultimately, reframing dollar-cost averaging as a spiritual practice elevates it from a technical tactic to a holistic discipline—a practice that marries financial acumen with psychological resilience and philosophical depth. It calls on investors to honour the passage of time, regulate emotional impulses, and embrace investing as a sustained commitment rather than episodic pursuit. This transformation is particularly vital in the crypto sphere, where rapid change and uncertainty abound.

By internalising DCA's deeper significance, investors gain more than market exposure; they cultivate a mindset attuned to growth, patience, and thoughtful engagement. The discipline to invest steadily, regardless of external noise, becomes a powerful form of agency—anchoring the investor amidst the market's storms and guiding them toward enduring success.

How to Think in Decades, Not Days-

In the frenetic world of cryptocurrency, where headlines shift by the hour and market swings can double or halve asset values within days, the ability to think in decades rather than days emerges as a defining skill—yet one rarely cultivated. This chapter advocates for a strategic patience that resists the seductive allure of short-term trends and market noise. It challenges readers to develop investment theses grounded not in the ephemeral but in enduring fundamentals, thus reclaiming time as the ultimate ally in wealth creation. Within the crypto space, patience itself stands as a rare and valuable asset, often eclipsing technical knowledge or market timing.

The temptation to react immediately to every price movement or hype cycle is understandable. Human cognition evolved to respond rapidly to perceived threats and opportunities, privileging immediacy. In contrast, crypto's nascent and volatile ecosystem amplifies these impulses, making impulsive decisions appear rational. Yet, as countless market downturns have demonstrated, reactionary investing typically erodes capital rather than grows it. Long-term thinking counters this cycle by embedding investing within a framework of deliberate, sustained engagement—anchoring decisions in vision rather than volatility.

Developing a long-term thesis begins with reframing time itself. Investors must shift perspective from daily charts and fleeting headlines to multi-year, even decade-spanning narratives. This approach entails identifying structural trends—such as blockchain adoption, regulatory evolution, or technological innovation—that transcend short-term noise. For example, viewing Bitcoin not as a speculative ticker but as a digital store of value maturing over decades fundamentally alters one's engagement. Similarly, recognising Ethereum's potential as a foundational layer for decentralised applications invites patience as the ecosystem evolves, rather than demands instant gratification.

Such temporal recalibration is best supported by mental models that clarify enduring value propositions. One effective model is the "S-curve" of technological adoption, which maps initial innovation through growth, maturity, and saturation phases. Early investors must tolerate volatility and uncertainty as part of the nascent growth phase, resisting the urge to exit prematurely. Another model emphasises competitive moats—the unique advantages that enable certain projects to maintain long-term relevance amid innovation and disruption. Discernment of these moats requires rigorous research beyond superficial market sentiment, anchoring investment theses in sustainable differentiation.

Long-term thinking also entails an ethical and philosophical dimension. Patience in crypto investing aligns with broader virtues of temperance, foresight, and humility. The investor is called to accept uncertainty, relinquish control over unpredictable markets, and focus instead on consistent principles and behaviours. This mindset parallels contemplative practices that value process over immediate outcomes, fostering resilience against anxiety induced by market turbulence. In doing so, patience becomes not passive inertia but an active, disciplined stance—an intentional choice to steward capital thoughtfully over time.

Yet adopting this outlook is not without tension. Crypto's rapid innovation cycles and evolving narratives continuously challenge static theses. Investors must balance conviction with adaptability, updating models as fundamental shifts emerge while resisting reactionary impulses. This dynamic balance requires ongoing learning and critical analysis, ensuring that long-term perspectives remain relevant and informed rather than dogmatic. The discipline to endure is complemented by the humility to revise, a hallmark of sophisticated investing.

Historical precedents offer instructive lessons. The dot-com bubble of the late 1990s exemplifies the perils of short-term euphoria followed by precipitous collapse. Conversely, investors who held stakes in transformative companies like Amazon or Google through volatile early years ultimately reaped substantial rewards. Crypto parallels these trajectories, underscoring the value of a long-term horizon in filtering transient speculation from sustainable innovation. The capacity to withstand interim setbacks distinguishes successful investors from mere gamblers.

Moreover, thinking in decades reframes portfolio construction. Rather than chasing every hot token or fleeting trend, investors prioritise assets aligned with long-term convictions and personal values. This approach encourages diversification across projects that collectively express a coherent worldview rather than fragmented market opportunism. Investment becomes autobiographical, reflecting one's beliefs about technology, society, and the future economy. Such alignment reinforces commitment and psychological endurance, critical for navigating crypto's inevitable volatility.

Practical strategies support this mindset. Setting clear investment goals with multi-year timeframes, automating contributions through mechanisms like dollar-cost averaging, and limiting portfolio monitoring frequency reduce emotional reactivity. Tools that facilitate disciplined, gradual engagement mitigate the temptation to act on short-term impulses. Additionally, adopting a "pause before acting" routine creates cognitive space for reflection, countering impulsive decisions driven by hype or fear.

The rarity of patience as an asset in crypto cannot be overstated. In an ecosystem where narratives evolve rapidly and social media amplifies immediacy, cultivating a long-term perspective is countercultural. Yet it is precisely this countercultural stance that unlocks enduring value. Patience allows investors to transcend the noise, to anchor themselves in fundamental truths rather than transient hype, and to harness the compounding power of time. It transforms investing from speculation to strategy, from reaction to intention.

Ultimately, thinking in decades rather than days demands a radical reorientation of how investors relate to markets, time, and themselves. It requires the intellectual discipline to develop and maintain robust theses, the emotional fortitude to withstand volatility, and the philosophical acceptance of uncertainty. By embracing this mindset, investors not only enhance their prospects of financial success but also cultivate a deeper, more sustainable relationship with their capital and the unfolding future of crypto.

Building a Portfolio That Reflects Your Life, Not Just the Market-

The act of investing, at its most profound level, is a mirror reflecting the individual investor's values, aspirations, and circumstances—not merely a transactional engagement with fluctuating markets. Yet, in the frenetic world of crypto, many find themselves ensnared by external narratives, chasing portfolios shaped by market trends or popular influencers rather than their own distinct life path. This subchapter asserts that building a portfolio aligned with one's lifestyle and personal vision is not only more sustainable but essential for meaningful, long-term success. Investing ceases to be a mere financial exercise and becomes, instead, an autobiographical journey.

The prevailing culture of investment advice often champions generic "best practices," algorithmic diversification, or momentum-based strategies. While these may have statistical validity, they risk divorcing the investor from their unique context: financial goals, risk tolerance, ethical considerations, and temporal horizons. Crypto, with its extraordinary volatility and social dynamism, demands a heightened awareness of this gap. *Portfolio construction without self-reflection is susceptible to external shocks and internal dissonance,* often leading to poor decision-making driven by anxiety, envy, or misinformation.

At the core of this philosophy is the recognition that financial assets carry narratives far beyond price movements. Each holding embodies a worldview—a bet on technology, governance, privacy, or societal change. For instance, an investor committed to decentralisation and digital sovereignty may prioritise assets like Bitcoin or privacy-focused tokens, accepting volatility as part of their ideological commitment. Conversely, a cautious individual with shorter-term goals may favour stablecoins or vetted institutional platforms. Both choices are valid, but their coherence with the investor's life story is what sustains discipline and resilience through market cycles.

To construct such a portfolio, investors must undertake rigorous self-inquiry. What are your financial goals over five, ten, or twenty years? How much volatility can you truly endure without abandoning your plan? What values—whether environmental sustainability, privacy, or innovation—do you want your capital to support? This introspection enables *investment as intentional expression*, where portfolio decisions integrate seamlessly with one's broader life narrative rather than fragmenting it.

Practical application of this ethos often involves tailoring asset allocation to life phases and responsibilities. A young professional with a high risk tolerance and time horizon may allocate aggressively toward emergent DeFi protocols or NFTs that resonate with their digital culture engagement. A mid-career individual prioritising wealth preservation for family obligations might emphasise Bitcoin and diversified stablecoins. Meanwhile, a retiree may focus on stable, income-generating crypto derivatives or tokenised real estate aligned with conservative financial management. These allocations are not dictated by market fads but by *living realities* and future aspirations.

The autobiographical approach also invites ethical and philosophical reflection. Unlike traditional assets, many crypto projects explicitly embody ideological frameworks—decentralisation, open access, censorship resistance—that resonate deeply with personal identity. Choosing to invest is, therefore, a statement of belief as much as a financial act. Aligning holdings with these beliefs fosters congruence and mitigates the psychological strain of market downturns, because losses or gains are situated within a meaningful context. Investors who perceive their portfolios as extensions of themselves demonstrate higher commitment and measured reactions to volatility.

Moreover, constructing a life-aligned portfolio necessitates ongoing adaptation. Life circumstances, goals, and values evolve, and so must investment strategies. This dynamic process calls for continuous education, self-awareness, and humility. Rigidity in portfolio design risks alienation from personal realities, while excessive reaction to short-term market noise leads to erratic decision-making. The investor's task is to balance constancy with flexibility, preserving core convictions while remaining open to revision as the external environment and inner world shift.

Case studies illuminate the power of this perspective. Consider the investor who channels their passion for renewable energy into blockchain projects focused on green energy credits or carbon trading. Their portfolio not only serves financial aims but amplifies personal commitment to sustainability. Contrast this with the investor swayed by viral hype, who diversifies indiscriminately across tokens detached from their values or risk tolerance, often resulting in disillusionment. The difference lies in narrative coherence—one portfolio tells a story that the investor inhabits; the other is a collage of disconnected hopes.

To translate this philosophy into practice, investors might begin by drafting a "personal investment manifesto"—a clear articulation of goals, values, risk appetite, and preferred technologies or sectors. This manifesto serves as a compass against which prospective investments are measured, filtering out noise and pressure. Equally important is developing rituals that reinforce alignment, such as periodic portfolio reviews not just for performance but for congruence with life changes, and reflective journaling to track emotional responses to market events.

Finally, embracing portfolio construction as autobiographical transforms the investor's relationship with capital. Wealth becomes not an end but a tool for self-expression, influence, and legacy. The portfolio's evolution charts personal growth, shifting priorities, and deepening understanding. This holistic view cultivates patience and equanimity, equipping investors to navigate the volatility of crypto markets with a grounded sense of purpose.

In sum, building a portfolio that reflects one's life demands a synthesis of financial acumen, self-knowledge, and ethical clarity. It challenges investors to step beyond market mimicry and embrace investing as a deliberate act of identity and intention. Such portfolios are not only more resilient but profoundly rewarding, aligning wealth creation with the authentic narrative of the individual behind the wallet.

Chapter 9
Taxes, Staking, and Territorial Realities

Taxation, so often relegated to the realm of drudgery or tolerated as a bureaucratic burden, takes on a different weight within the world of crypto. Here it is not simply paperwork or obligation, but a revealing test of sovereignty and strategic awareness. To grapple with tax law is to confront, head-on, the frameworks that shape one's financial existence. It is less about ticking boxes for the state and more about recognising how power and autonomy meet in the language of compliance. Fear—so common in this domain—drives avoidance, procrastination, or worse, costly missteps. Yet once understood with clarity, tax ceases to be a lurking threat and instead becomes a tool, a foundation upon which confidence and control can be built.

Alongside the subject of taxation sits the equally charged issue of staking—a mechanism wrapped in the language of yield and ease, promising stability in a turbulent market. But beneath its polished surface lies a harder truth: staking is a pact, an exchange of flexibility for reward. The very act of locking assets that promise "passive income" also risks tethering the investor, leaving them bound when agility is most needed. This chapter insists on a sober reckoning with staking: not to dismiss its potential, but to examine its risks, its limits, and its place within a portfolio that reflects real personal aims rather than market slogans.

Geography, meanwhile, intrudes in ways the digital imagination often forgets. We like to think of crypto as borderless, yet every jurisdiction stamps its authority differently. Taxation regimes, compliance expectations, even the interpretation of decentralised finance vary sharply between the United States, Canada, the United Kingdom, India, Australia, and beyond. In this way, where one lives is no trivial backdrop but a decisive element of strategy. National context is law made personal, and any investor blind to this fact courts unnecessary risk. Mastery of crypto therefore requires not only market literacy but also legal and territorial awareness.

Threading through all of this is a recurring imperative: never to outsource understanding entirely. By all means, lean on accountants, advisors, and legal experts; prudence demands it. But hand over comprehension itself, and you hand over power. Literacy in your own financial story—knowing the why as well as the what of tax choices, staking decisions, and jurisdictional constraints—is itself a form of security. Passive compliance breeds fragility; active understanding fosters resilience.

The reader who follows this argument will come away not merely with technical instruction, but with an altered stance. Tax becomes not a shadow but a lens; staking shifts from shiny promise to nuanced instrument; geography transforms from background fact to central force. The chapter's aim is less to issue commandments than to cultivate a mindset: one of responsibility, foresight, and deliberate agency.

Through comparative examples, reflective inquiry, and practical grounding, the text insists that taxes, staking, and jurisdiction are not side notes in the score but part of the central melody of crypto life. They are the places where choice collides with structure, where autonomy encounters authority. To engage them seriously is to move from reaction into design, from fear into clarity. In this sense, compliance is not defeat but strategy, and geography not constraint but context. For the thoughtful investor, these are not burdens to endure, but tools—sometimes heavy, sometimes awkward—that, when properly wielded, make the edifice of a durable, ethical, and sovereign crypto portfolio possible.

Tax Isn't Boring—It's Existential-

Tax is often dismissed as a mundane obligation, a tedious chore to be postponed or avoided, particularly in the volatile, fast-moving world of cryptocurrency. Yet this perspective obscures a deeper truth: tax law is not merely a bureaucratic inconvenience but a fundamental arena where personal sovereignty, strategic clarity, and ethical agency converge. For those who engage with crypto as a long-term venture, understanding tax is less about compliance and more about shaping one's financial identity and navigating the complex interface between individual freedom and societal structure.

The fear of taxation is widespread—and understandable. The crypto space is rife with uncertainty: evolving regulations, jurisdictional discrepancies, and frequent legal ambiguities create fertile ground for anxiety. This fear often manifests as avoidance, whether through incomplete reporting, reliance on shady schemes, or outright ignorance. However, such avoidance does not erase obligation; it merely postpones consequences and increases vulnerability. *Fear, left unexamined, leads to paralysis and poor decision-making.*

Conversely, clarity around tax obligations is a form of empowerment. It provides a framework within which one can make conscious, informed choices rather than reactive, impulsive moves. Understanding the tax implications of buying, selling, staking, or gifting crypto turns compliance into strategy—an opportunity to optimise outcomes, reduce risk, and assert control. *This strategic clarity transforms tax from an adversary into a tool of financial sovereignty.*

The existential nature of tax becomes clearer when we consider that tax law effectively defines the rules of participation in a society's economic life. It delineates what wealth means in practice—not just as a number on a screen, but as an accountable, socially embedded resource. Navigating tax law is thus an act of citizenship and self-governance, requiring both awareness and responsibility. In this sense, mastery of tax codes is a prerequisite for exercising true autonomy within the modern financial ecosystem.

Consider the example of crypto investors in the United States, where the IRS treats cryptocurrency as property, subject to capital gains tax. This classification means every transaction—selling, trading, even using crypto for purchases—has taxable consequences. An investor unaware of these details risks costly mistakes, while one equipped with knowledge can plan trades to leverage favourable tax treatments, such as long-term capital gains rates. This is not merely a technicality but a fundamental component of financial literacy that distinguishes successful, sustainable investment from reckless speculation.

Internationally, tax treatments vary dramatically. Countries like Germany and Portugal offer lenient regimes for long-term crypto holdings, while others impose stringent reporting requirements and high rates. Understanding these territorial realities is crucial, especially for individuals with cross-border activities or dual citizenship. The choice of residence, legal domicile, or business registration can radically alter one's tax exposure, underscoring tax's intimate link to personal sovereignty and strategic decision-making.

The complexity of tax law, especially within crypto, also reveals a profound ethical dimension. Transparency, accurate reporting, and timely payment are acts that sustain the collective infrastructure enabling markets and public goods. At the same time, taxpayers must negotiate the tension between civic duty and protecting their rights and assets. This balance demands not blind obedience, but critical engagement and principled navigation—a nuanced ethical practice that elevates tax beyond mere obligation.

Technological innovation in crypto has also introduced new tax challenges and opportunities. Decentralised finance (DeFi), non-fungible tokens (NFTs), and staking protocols create transactions and income streams that traditional tax frameworks struggle to classify and regulate. The resulting grey areas necessitate not only legal awareness but also active participation in shaping emerging tax policies. Investors who cultivate tax literacy position themselves to influence this evolving landscape and defend their interests effectively.

At the personal level, tax clarity fosters peace of mind. It dissolves the cognitive burden of uncertainty and the looming threat of penalties. Moreover, it encourages deliberate investment choices aligned with one's financial goals and values rather than emotional reactions to market noise or tax panic. This disciplined approach enhances resilience in a notoriously volatile environment, cultivating patience and foresight.

In sum, tax in crypto is not a peripheral, dull subject but a central pillar of strategic investing and personal empowerment. To approach it with curiosity and rigor is to embrace a vital aspect of digital financial citizenship. By transforming fear into knowledge, avoidance into engagement, and confusion into clarity, investors claim agency over their wealth and their future. This shift—from dread to mastery—is not only prudent but essential for anyone seeking to thrive in the complex, dynamic world of cryptocurrencies.

Staking: Yield or Trap?

The allure of staking in the cryptocurrency world is undeniable. Promises of passive income, compounding yields, and participation in network security invite investors to commit their assets with the prospect of earning rewards beyond mere price appreciation. Yet staking is not a simple proposition of risk-free gain; it is a nuanced practice, an exchange of liquidity and control for yield, fraught with technical, financial, and psychological implications. Understanding what staking *gives* and what it *locks* is essential before committing capital. To stake with eyes wide open is to engage in a disciplined negotiation between opportunity and constraint, agency and surrender.

At its core, staking involves locking up tokens to support a blockchain's operation—validating transactions, securing consensus, or powering decentralised applications—in return for a share of the network's rewards. This mechanism, integral to Proof of Stake (PoS) blockchains such as Ethereum 2.0, Cardano, and Solana, replaces the energy-intensive mining of Proof of Work with economic incentives aligned to ownership. The financial appeal is straightforward: by staking, holders earn yield, typically expressed as an annual percentage rate (APR), which can considerably enhance long-term returns compared to simple holding.

Yet this financial benefit is inseparable from a set of constraints and risks that are too often overlooked. The tokens staked are frequently illiquid for defined periods, sometimes extending for months or even years. This lockup period can be perilous in volatile markets, where the opportunity cost of capital may be significant. If the market price of the token plummets, stakers cannot readily exit to mitigate losses. Conversely, if more lucrative opportunities arise, staked assets cannot be redeployed swiftly. This dynamic introduces a strategic trade-off: yield versus flexibility.

Moreover, staking exposes investors to technical risks. Validator nodes can be penalised or "slashed" for misbehaviour, downtime, or failure to adhere to network protocols, resulting in partial or total loss of staked assets. While such penalties are designed to ensure network integrity, they create a dimension of operational risk uncommon in traditional asset classes. Stakers relying on third-party custodians or staking-as-a-service providers face additional counterparty risk, necessitating due diligence akin to that required for choosing a financial institution or fund manager.

Beyond the tangible financial and operational considerations lies a deeper, psychological dimension. Staking demands a posture of patience and conviction that can conflict with the emotional volatility of investing. Locking away assets can provoke anxiety and second-guessing, particularly during market downturns or when news cycles amplify fear. The discipline to resist impulsive unstaking or panic selling is itself a skill, intertwined with emotional regulation as much as market savvy.

Consider Ethereum's transition to PoS with the launch of the Beacon Chain and eventual merge, a watershed moment in crypto history. Early stakers committed significant ETH into a smart contract, unable to withdraw for an extended period. Those who embraced this commitment anticipated the long-term ecological and economic benefits of PoS, accepting short-term illiquidity for systemic advantages. Yet many newcomers, enticed by advertised yields, underestimated the complexities—lockup durations, withdrawal delays, and the evolving nature of staking rewards—leading to disappointment or confusion. This real-world example underscores the necessity of informed engagement rather than impulsive participation.

The conversation around staking must also confront its economic sustainability. High staking yields in nascent projects can be a function of inflationary tokenomics, diluting value over time. Investors must discern whether yields stem from genuine network utility and demand or are incentivised artificially to attract capital. Staking, therefore, is not merely a financial exercise but a critical appraisal of a project's design, governance, and long-term viability.

Additionally, the decentralisation ethos central to many crypto projects is both advanced and challenged by staking. While staking can promote security and community participation, concentration of stakes in a few large validators or pools can undermine decentralisation. Investors must be mindful of how their staking choices influence the broader ecosystem, balancing personal gain against collective health.

From a practical standpoint, the myriad staking options—from self-managed validators requiring technical expertise to custodial services offering ease but with inherent trust trade-offs—demand careful selection. Each choice reflects different risk tolerances, resource commitments, and philosophical stances on control versus convenience. This diversity of pathways illustrates that staking is not a monolith but a spectrum of strategies suited to distinct investor profiles.

In sum, staking is a compelling, multifaceted tool that, when used judiciously, can enhance portfolio returns and deepen engagement with blockchain networks. However, it is neither a guaranteed profit machine nor a casual endeavour. The decision to stake must be grounded in a clear-eyed understanding of what is surrendered alongside what is gained: liquidity, flexibility, autonomy, and risk exposure. Embracing this complexity, rather than simplifying or ignoring it, equips investors to stake with informed confidence—transforming a potential trap into a deliberate, strategic opportunity.

Geography Is Policy: Crypto Across Borders-

Cryptocurrency, by design, transcends national borders, promising a new form of financial sovereignty untethered from traditional state controls. Yet despite this inherent borderlessness, the reality of crypto investing and utilisation is deeply embedded within the jurisdictional frameworks of nation-states. *Geography is policy*—your location shapes the regulatory environment you navigate, the risks you face, and the freedoms you can exercise. Understanding how different countries treat crypto is not a peripheral curiosity but a central element of strategic decision-making for any serious participant in the space.

Take the United States, where the regulatory landscape is complex and often contradictory. Crypto assets are simultaneously classified as property by the Internal Revenue Service (IRS), commodities by the Commodity Futures Trading Commission (CFTC), and securities in certain contexts by the Securities and Exchange Commission (SEC). This patchwork regulatory environment creates significant uncertainty for investors and enterprises alike. For example, the SEC's aggressive stance on initial coin offerings (ICOs) and decentralized finance (DeFi) protocols has chilled some innovation while prompting legal scrutiny. Meanwhile, tax reporting obligations are stringent, with capital gains taxes applying to crypto transactions in ways that can surprise unwary holders. The US represents a paradox: an innovation hub constrained by regulatory complexity, where freedom to innovate wrestles with institutional caution.

Canada offers a contrasting model, blending relatively progressive attitudes with prudent regulation. The Canadian Securities Administrators have issued clearer guidelines on crypto asset classifications, and the country has become home to a number of regulated exchanges that operate under established securities laws. Moreover, Canada's tax authority treats cryptocurrency as a commodity, with capital gains tax applied on disposals, yet there is an emphasis on clarity and taxpayer education. This regulatory steadiness provides a degree of certainty that facilitates both innovation and compliance. However, challenges remain, particularly around cross-border issues and the fragmented provincial regulatory framework. Investors in Canada benefit from a comparatively balanced environment but must still navigate nuances inherent to a federated system.

Across the Atlantic, the United Kingdom presents a regulatory environment that has evolved rapidly post-Brexit. The Financial Conduct Authority (FCA) has positioned itself as a proactive regulator, implementing robust anti-money laundering (AML) measures and requiring crypto businesses to register and adhere to stringent controls. The UK's approach reflects a willingness to integrate crypto into the existing financial ecosystem, emphasising consumer protection without stifling innovation. Tax treatment classifies crypto as property subject to capital gains tax, yet the government has explored introducing more comprehensive crypto-friendly regulations to foster fintech growth. This evolving framework positions the UK as a competitive yet cautious jurisdiction, where strategic clarity demands continuous engagement with regulatory developments.

India's treatment of cryptocurrency is emblematic of a jurisdiction grappling with the tension between control and innovation. After periods of uncertainty—including an outright banking ban on crypto transactions that was later overturned—the government has shifted towards a more ambivalent stance. Recent legislative proposals suggest a tough regulatory approach, including taxation regimes that impose a flat 30% tax on crypto gains and stringent reporting requirements. The Reserve Bank of India's cautious posture reflects broader concerns about financial stability and illicit activity. For crypto investors in India, this creates a high-risk environment characterised by legal ambiguities and policy flux, where the cost of participation includes navigating potential prohibitions and heavy taxation.

Australia offers another example of pragmatic regulation, blending encouragement for fintech innovation with robust oversight. The Australian Securities and Investments Commission (ASIC) regulates crypto exchanges under existing financial services laws, requiring licensing and consumer protections. Tax treatment aligns with global norms, treating crypto as property subject to capital gains tax. Importantly, Australia has sought to provide clear guidance and has fostered an ecosystem where innovation can thrive under defined rules. This regulatory clarity enhances investor confidence and promotes sustainable growth, illustrating how jurisdictional policy can enable both security and freedom.

These jurisdictions illustrate that *where* you operate or invest in crypto profoundly shapes your experience. Regulatory certainty, tax policy, and enforcement priorities differ substantially, influencing transaction costs, legal risks, and opportunities for innovation. Geography is more than mere location; it is an axis of policy that governs access, limits, and privileges in the crypto world.

Beyond regulation, geopolitical factors also shape crypto realities. For instance, countries with capital controls or unstable fiat currencies often see crypto as a refuge or alternative store of value, while others view it as a threat to monetary sovereignty. This dynamic fuels both adoption and repression, underscoring that the interplay between state policy and crypto is deeply political as well as economic.

For the discerning investor or operator, understanding these territorial realities is vital. The temptation to view crypto as uniformly borderless must be tempered by appreciation of how local laws, cultural attitudes, and institutional capabilities mediate that freedom. Knowledge of one's regulatory environment transforms anxiety into strategic clarity, allowing for proactive compliance, risk management, and opportunity identification.

Moreover, globalisation does not eliminate jurisdictional risk—it redistributes it. Cross-border transactions, custody arrangements, and decentralized finance expose participants to multi-jurisdictional compliance demands and enforcement risks. A well-rounded crypto strategy incorporates this complexity, recognising that digital assets live simultaneously in code and law, innovation and regulation.

Ultimately, the lesson is that *crypto freedom* is not an abstract ideal but a pragmatic negotiation with geographic realities. Knowing how your country of residence or operation treats crypto allows you to calibrate your participation in ways that preserve sovereignty while mitigating exposure. This territorial literacy is indispensable for anyone seeking not only to survive but to thrive in the evolving global crypto ecosystem.

Don't Outsource What You Must Understand-

In the landscape of cryptocurrency, where complexity and novelty often breed uncertainty, the impulse to delegate responsibility—to financial advisors, tax professionals, or legal experts—is understandable, even prudent. Yet, *outsourcing without comprehension* is a vulnerability cloaked in convenience. The core truth is stark: no matter how capable your advisors, *you* must be literate in your own financial story. Personal sovereignty in crypto demands more than passive trust; it requires active understanding. Without this foundation, delegation morphs into abdication, exposing you to risks far beyond missed opportunities or regulatory penalties.

The allure of expert guidance is undeniable. Crypto tax law is labyrinthine, jurisdictionally fragmented, and evolving at a pace that often outstrips traditional frameworks. Staking protocols, DeFi instruments, and NFT marketplaces introduce layers of technical and legal complexity that can overwhelm even seasoned investors. Hiring professionals to navigate these waters can save time and shield against errors. However, the efficacy of this delegation rests squarely on the client's capacity to grasp fundamental principles and decisions—if you do not understand what you are delegating, you cannot effectively oversee or evaluate the advice received.

Consider the phenomenon of regulatory compliance failures stemming from ignorance rather than malfeasance. In several high-profile cases, individuals faced crippling tax audits or legal sanctions not because their accountants acted negligently, but because the clients failed to provide accurate, complete information or to comprehend the implications of transactions. The client's lack of literacy transformed an advisory relationship into a liability. This underscores a vital lesson: *financial literacy is the scaffolding that supports responsible delegation.* It is not a luxury but a necessity.

Moreover, the crypto ecosystem itself demands a distinctive form of literacy. Traditional finance operates within well-established regulatory boundaries and reporting mechanisms. Crypto, by contrast, often exists in legal grey zones, with tax treatments varying widely by country and transaction type. This ambiguity requires investors to understand not just the numbers, but the narrative: what constitutes taxable events, how staking rewards are classified, or how cross-border transactions impact reporting obligations. This narrative comprehension allows you to anticipate questions, scrutinise advice, and adapt to regulatory changes. In this context, *knowledge is both armour and compass.*

Delegation without understanding also impairs strategic agility. Markets move swiftly, and opportunities or risks can emerge overnight. If you depend solely on external advisors who may be constrained by workload, expertise gaps, or conflicts of interest, your ability to respond is compromised. Conversely, a well-informed investor can engage meaningfully with advisors, ask probing questions, and make decisions aligned with personal risk tolerance and long-term goals. This active partnership transcends transactional relationships, forging a collaborative dynamic essential for navigating crypto's unique volatility and innovation cycles.

Beyond practicalities, there is an ethical dimension to financial literacy in crypto. The sector champions decentralisation, individual empowerment, and disruption of opaque institutions. Surrendering understanding to intermediaries runs counter to this ethos. It risks replicating the very vulnerabilities—information asymmetry, misaligned incentives, opacity—that crypto seeks to dismantle. *Owning your financial narrative is a manifestation of the sovereignty that defines crypto's promise.* It is an act of integrity, self-respect, and alignment with the movement's foundational values.

Real-world examples further illustrate the stakes. The collapse of certain DeFi protocols or centralised exchanges has led to widespread losses for investors who lacked insight into the underlying smart contracts, security risks, or custodian practices. In many cases, these losses were exacerbated by misplaced trust in third parties without sufficient personal due diligence. While professional advice is indispensable, it cannot substitute for *the investor's own vigilance and understanding.* This vigilance entails continuous learning—engaging with whitepapers, regulatory updates, and community discourse to remain informed.

Finally, embracing literacy does not imply mastering every technical detail but cultivating a framework of understanding that enables sound questions and informed decisions. It means recognising the limits of expertise, seeking clarity when in doubt, and integrating advice into a coherent personal strategy. *This disciplined engagement transforms delegation from blind trust into empowered partnership,* minimising vulnerabilities and maximising resilience in a landscape defined by uncertainty.

In sum, the adage "don't outsource what you must understand" is not a cautionary cliché but a strategic imperative. Crypto's promise of personal financial sovereignty is attainable only when coupled with informed agency. Delegating without comprehension is not freedom—it is a different form of dependence. For those committed to thriving in this evolving space, *financial literacy is the first and most enduring investment.*

Chapter 10
Quiet Wealth in a Loud World

In a culture awash with spectacle and ceaseless display, the very notion of wealth has grown louder—gaudy, performative, endlessly paraded before the public eye. Social media, of course, fans the flames: timelines drip with ostentation, portfolios are flaunted as though trophies, and crypto is no exception. Every moonshot, every viral gain, is broadcast with a kind of manic insistence. Yet what passes for strength in this carnival of visibility is often little more than noise. True power, more often than not, resides in silence. This chapter urges a reorientation: to think of wealth not as a performance staged for others, but as a private achievement, carefully tended and intentionally veiled. Quiet wealth is the unseen flex—an act of sovereignty, of calm stewardship, of mastery over the impulse to impress.

In such a frame, privacy ceases to be mere defence. It becomes agency. The capacity to accumulate quietly, to move unseen, to sidestep the corrosive theatre of comparison, is itself a form of strength. Here lies the paradox: the less you reveal, the more control you command. Anonymity, discretion, and the discipline to resist spectacle build a sanctuary where wealth can endure untouched by envy, predation, or distraction. In a world of immediacy and exposure, such restraint is both countercultural and profoundly liberating.

Yet discretion alone is not the full measure of quiet wealth. Holding, so often trivialised by memes and the hollow cry of "HODL," deserves to be recast—not as passive inertia but as active stewardship. To hold is not to sleepwalk through volatility; it is to assume guardianship across seasons, to shoulder the responsibility of carrying value forward. That act requires resolve, patience, and a deliberate sense of what merits preservation. In this light, holding is less about resisting panic than about embodying resilience—an art that grows rarer by the day.

Still, wealth is never only private. It lives within social contexts, and here discretion demands another layer: knowing what to say, and perhaps more importantly, when to say nothing. To reveal one's holdings indiscriminately is not simply careless; it can be dangerous. Communication, in this sense, is strategy. The way you speak—or refrain—about crypto shapes trust, protects relationships, and insulates against risk. To cultivate such social intelligence is to understand that silence, tact, and calibrated disclosure are not evasions but instruments of sovereignty.

From here the chapter turns back to something more fundamental: intention. Crypto may dazzle with speed, but beneath the rush lies a deeper question—what does any of this serve? It is easy to forget why one began, easier still to lose sight of what matters beyond the numbers. Revisiting those first motives, testing them against present reality, anchoring them to future purpose—this is not indulgence. It is design. Quiet wealth, in the end, is not a final destination but a condition of life lived with coherence, where financial choices are braided into one's values, aspirations, and legacy.

The journey mapped here is both pragmatic and philosophical. It charts privacy as power, stewardship as discipline, communication as armour, and reflection as compass. In a clamorous world where wealth is measured by how loudly it shouts, this chapter closes with a different proposition: that silence itself can be a form of strength, and discretion a kind of freedom. Wealth, when lived quietly, is not diminished. It is intensified. It becomes less about what others see, and more about what endures.

The Invisible Flex: Privacy as Power

In an age where every move can be broadcast instantly, the decision to remain private—especially about one's wealth—emerges as a radical act of power. The allure of public acclaim, the validation of likes, and the adrenaline of exposure seduce many to showcase their financial successes, yet the most profound form of influence is often that which goes unseen. *Privacy is not merely a defensive shield; it is an assertion of autonomy, a deliberate cultivation of strength through discretion.* This principle resonates deeply in the cryptocurrency realm, where anonymity is woven into the very fabric of the technology, yet the culture frequently gravitates toward performative displays. The tension between these impulses reveals that *real power is quiet*—a form of wealth accumulation untethered from spectacle and grounded in sovereign control.

The first layer of this quiet power is anonymity itself. Unlike traditional finance, where identities are linked irrevocably to assets, many crypto protocols allow for pseudonymity or, at the very least, control over what is disclosed. This means that individuals can *accumulate value without the attendant vulnerabilities of public scrutiny.* Anonymity safeguards against a variety of risks: from theft and extortion to social pressures and psychological burdens that accompany public wealth. Yet, the value of anonymity transcends mere security. It fosters *a state of mental freedom*—a space where decisions are made without the distortion of external expectations or the compulsion to perform. This mental clarity, often overlooked in mainstream conversations, is a critical advantage in managing wealth sustainably over the long term.

At its core, this invisible flex challenges dominant narratives that equate wealth with ostentation. Cultural pressures—especially in digital communities—push individuals to showcase gains, position themselves as "influencers," and chase ephemeral status markers. Yet such performativity can become a trap, exposing one to increased risk and emotional volatility. The act of *low-profile accumulation* counters this by emphasising patience, humility, and a focus on intrinsic rather than extrinsic value. It is a rejection of the cult of immediacy and an embrace of *strategic silence* that allows wealth to grow organically and discreetly. This posture not only protects assets but also cultivates resilience against the distractions and manipulations endemic to hyperconnected societies.

Beyond the tactical benefits, embracing privacy entails a profound spiritual detachment from performance culture. The ceaseless demand to broadcast success can erode one's sense of self, tethering identity to external approval and market fluctuations. The invisible flex, however, cultivates a *quiet confidence* that anchors identity in enduring values rather than transient applause. This detachment is not indifference but a conscious choice to prioritise *long-term well-being over short-term gratification.* It aligns with philosophies that value mindfulness and intentionality, situating financial practice within a broader context of personal sovereignty and inner peace.

Yet, the challenge remains: how to navigate the paradox that cryptocurrency itself is a public ledger, inherently transparent and auditable. While blockchains provide pseudonymity, they do not guarantee anonymity without deliberate effort. Here, *technical literacy becomes indispensable.* Understanding privacy tools such as mixers, privacy coins, and off-chain storage is crucial to maintaining discretion. Moreover, the psychological discipline to avoid broadcasting one's holdings or intentions is equally vital. The invisible flex requires not just technological savvy but *a culture of restraint*—a commitment to letting wealth speak through stability and endurance rather than noise.

Examining real-world applications highlights the potency of this approach. Consider high-net-worth individuals who deliberately maintain low public profiles, opting to safeguard their crypto holdings offline or distribute assets among multiple cold wallets. Their strategy often includes *eschewing social media bragging* and maintaining minimalist digital footprints. This approach mitigates risks and reduces psychological stress, allowing wealth to function as *a foundation for freedom rather than a burden of expectation.* Similarly, communities that prioritise privacy—whether through encrypted communication or decentralized governance—demonstrate how anonymity fosters trust and long-term cooperation absent performative distractions.

Contrastingly, the perils of public performance in crypto are stark. High-profile hacks, social engineering attacks, and publicised rug pulls disproportionately affect those who disclose holdings or strategies widely. Public visibility can invite targeted harassment, regulatory scrutiny, and market manipulation. Moreover, the cultural compulsion to engage in 'showrooming' one's portfolio fuels speculation, anxiety, and short-termism, undermining the foundational ethos of decentralised finance. These dynamics reinforce that *privacy is not an afterthought but a strategic imperative.*

Ethically, embracing privacy also reflects respect for the wider community. In a system designed for decentralisation and peer-to-peer empowerment, maintaining discretion avoids signaling vulnerabilities that can destabilise markets or foster envy-driven conflict. It cultivates an environment where participants can operate from strength and discretion rather than exposure and defensiveness. The invisible flex, therefore, aligns individual interest with collective resilience, demonstrating how *privacy is both a personal and communal asset.*

The invisible flex extends beyond wealth to how one approaches influence and legacy. Quiet accumulation allows for deliberate stewardship, positioning wealth as a tool for *generational empowerment* rather than performative consumption. It invites reflection on what it means to wield influence responsibly, detached from the noise of social media and transient trends. This perspective reframes success as *an enduring contribution*—measured not by applause but by the stability and freedom one secures for oneself and others.

Ultimately, this subchapter argues that in a world increasingly driven by spectacle and transparency, *privacy emerges as the last bastion of personal sovereignty.* It challenges readers to reconsider their relationship with wealth and success, advocating for a posture of quiet strength that privileges long-term security over short-lived fame. The invisible flex is a disciplined practice—a way of inhabiting financial life that demands courage, wisdom, and restraint. For those who embrace it, privacy is not just a shield but a source of profound power and freedom, the foundation upon which lasting wealth is built.

From HODLing to Stewardship

The familiar rallying cry of "HODL" in cryptocurrency circles—originally a typo for "hold"—has evolved into a mantra symbolising steadfast commitment amid volatility. Yet, at its core, *HODLing often risks being misunderstood as passive endurance, a waiting game driven by hope or stubbornness rather than intentionality.* This subchapter invites readers to transcend this limited view and embrace *stewardship*: an active, conscientious guardianship of assets imbued with purpose and responsibility. Holding is not merely about resisting the urge to sell; it is about cultivating a dynamic relationship with one's holdings that aligns with a broader vision and ethical framework.

At first glance, the distinction between HODLing and stewardship may appear semantic. However, it represents a profound shift in mindset and practice. HODLing has historically been a defensive response to market turbulence, a psychological strategy to avoid panic-selling. While this has proven effective for many in accumulating wealth, it can also lead to passivity, detachment, and missed opportunities for meaningful engagement. Stewardship, by contrast, positions holding as an *active role—one that requires ongoing education, intentional decisions, and a commitment to the ecosystem that the assets represent.* This approach recognises that cryptocurrencies are not inert objects but components of evolving technological, economic, and social networks.

This reframing is essential because it challenges investors to see their holdings as *more than financial instruments—as legacies, as statements of values, as participation in a broader movement.* Stewardship entails embracing the ethical implications of one's investment choices. For example, holding Bitcoin is not just about potential appreciation; it is a vote for monetary sovereignty, decentralisation, and censorship resistance. Similarly, holding tokens in decentralised finance (DeFi) protocols or governance tokens in DAOs implicates investors in the health, governance, and future direction of those projects. Such perspectives demand a level of engagement and accountability absent from simple HODLing.

The real-world impact of adopting stewardship over passive holding is tangible. Consider early adopters who actively participated in governance processes, contributed to community initiatives, or supported educational efforts. Their engagement enriched not only their own understanding but also strengthened the protocols' resilience and adaptability. Conversely, passive holders may find themselves alienated from developments or vulnerable to market shifts driven by actors more deeply embedded in the ecosystem. Stewardship cultivates *agency and foresight*, empowering investors to navigate complexity rather than be buffeted by it.

Ethically, stewardship invites reflection on the relationship between wealth and responsibility. The allure of speculative gains can obscure the broader social and environmental footprint of crypto projects. Stewardship demands that investors *weigh their holdings against the values they espouse and the impact they wish to have.* This might involve divesting from projects with unsustainable energy consumption or supporting those with transparent governance and inclusive communities. Through stewardship, holding becomes a vehicle for *purposeful influence*, not just profit.

The psychological dimensions of this shift are equally significant. Passive HODLing can engender complacency or cognitive dissonance when market behaviour contradicts expectations. Stewardship, framed as an ongoing practice, fosters emotional resilience and intellectual curiosity. Investors learn to manage uncertainty through informed engagement rather than denial or detachment. This mindset aligns with principles of mindful investing, where *patience is coupled with vigilance and learning*. It transforms the holding experience into a journey of growth and adaptation.

From a practical standpoint, stewardship entails cultivating habits and structures that support long-term success. This includes regular portfolio review aligned with evolving goals, active participation in community governance when applicable, and maintaining security practices that protect assets. Stewardship also means preparing for transitions—whether market shifts, technological upgrades, or personal life changes—with intention and clarity. This proactive stance contrasts sharply with the reactive passivity that often accompanies unreflective holding.

Contrasting views arise around the feasibility and desirability of stewardship in a highly volatile, rapidly evolving market. Critics argue that constant engagement risks overtrading or succumbing to noise, undermining the benefits of patience. While this concern is valid, stewardship does not imply frenetic activity but *disciplined engagement*—a thoughtful balance of attention and restraint. It demands critical discernment: knowing when to act, when to listen, and when to wait. Stewardship thus refines the art of navigation amid uncertainty.

The cultural implications of stewardship are far-reaching. It challenges the dominant narratives of instant wealth and social signalling pervasive in crypto communities. By prioritising meaning over momentum, stewardship re-centres investment as a *form of craftsmanship*, where skill, ethics, and vision converge. This cultural shift has the potential to foster more sustainable, inclusive, and resilient ecosystems—ones that reward thoughtful participation rather than mere speculation.

Ultimately, embracing stewardship transforms the act of holding from a passive gamble into an expression of sovereignty and care. It invites investors to *see themselves as custodians of something greater than capital—a collective project of financial autonomy, technological innovation, and social transformation.* This perspective enriches the investment journey with depth and purpose, offering a path to wealth that honours both the individual and the community. The move from HODLing to stewardship is thus not just a strategy but a call to conscious, empowered investment in a world of possibility and risk.

How to Talk (or Not Talk) About Your Crypto

Navigating conversations about cryptocurrency is far from a casual social exercise; it is an exercise in social intelligence, personal security, and strategic communication. The decision of *who* to tell, *what* to reveal, and *when* to hold silence shapes not only your privacy but your very financial safety. In an environment rife with scams, envy, misinformation, and volatile market sentiment, *the act of talking about your crypto holdings is itself a security consideration.* This subchapter offers a nuanced exploration of interpersonal wisdom tailored for the crypto space, underscoring that silence is often as powerful a tool as speech.

The impulse to share financial success—or failure—is deeply human. Sharing can foster community, validate choices, and build networks. Yet in the crypto world, this impulse carries outsized risk. Stories abound of individuals targeted after casual disclosures on social media or even private chats. Digital footprints create vulnerabilities that traditional financial privacy once shielded. Thus, understanding *when sharing serves a purpose and when it becomes a liability* is a critical skill for any investor. This requires a mindset that recognises conversation as an act with consequences, not mere idle chatter.

Context is paramount. Revealing your crypto involvement to a trusted financial advisor who respects confidentiality is markedly different from posting your portfolio on a public forum. Even among friends or family, varying degrees of financial literacy and emotional maturity mean that disclosures can trigger misunderstanding, jealousy, or pressure. Consider the psychological dynamics: discussing crypto gains may unintentionally invite unwelcome advice, requests for loans, or even exploitation. Conversely, silence can shield you from these pressures, preserving autonomy and mental well-being.

The challenge lies in *striking a balance between openness and discretion.* Transparency is often celebrated in investment communities for fostering trust and collective learning. However, unfiltered transparency in crypto can be perilous. Security breaches frequently result from social engineering exploits that begin with seemingly innocuous personal information. Sharing too much can inadvertently arm bad actors. Thus, *social intelligence—the ability to read situations, anticipate reactions, and tailor disclosures—is a vital layer of security.*

This perspective reframes communication about crypto as a strategic practice. It invites reflection on the intentions behind sharing. Are you seeking advice, celebration, connection, or validation? Each motive suggests different levels of disclosure. When seeking expertise, carefully vetting interlocutors protects against misinformation and scams. When celebrating milestones, one might choose intimate circles rather than public arenas. Recognising these nuances enhances control over one's narrative and safeguards assets.

Moreover, this approach encourages cultivating an internal compass for privacy rather than relying on external validation. In crypto's fast-paced, performative culture, there is temptation to signal wealth or savvy. Yet, the most resilient investors often practice *digital minimalism*: revealing only what is necessary and cultivating detachment from external approval*. This detachment is not secrecy for secrecy's sake but a disciplined choice to preserve focus and security. It challenges the prevailing narrative that public exposure equals success.

Real-world examples illustrate these dynamics vividly. Cases where individuals were hacked or extorted following boastful posts serve as cautionary tales. Conversely, many who maintain a low profile, quietly managing their portfolios and engaging selectively, report greater peace of mind and fewer distractions. The lessons here transcend technical security measures, highlighting *the social dimension of digital asset protection.*

Contrasting cultural attitudes towards financial privacy further complicate this landscape. In some societies, discussing wealth openly is taboo; in others, it is a source of pride. Crypto investors operating globally must navigate these cultural contexts with sensitivity, tailoring their disclosures not only for security but for social harmony. This complexity underscores that *effective communication about crypto is as much about cultural fluency as it is about personal discretion.*

Ethically, this subchapter urges reflection on the responsibilities entailed in sharing. Oversharing can inadvertently fuel FOMO (fear of missing out), market speculation, or unethical behaviour among peers. Thoughtful communication considers the broader impact on community dynamics and market health. Stewardship extends to how one's narrative influences others, encouraging a culture of respect, humility, and prudence.

Ultimately, mastering the art of when and how to talk about crypto is *a practice of agency—an assertion of control over both financial and social domains.* It aligns with the broader theme of this book, which advocates for informed, intentional engagement with the crypto space. Social intelligence becomes a cornerstone of security, empowering investors to protect not only their wealth but their well-being and relationships.

The ability to navigate these conversations with discernment is a form of empowerment that complements technical safeguards. As crypto continues to permeate society, the skills of nuanced communication, strategic disclosure, and respectful silence will define those who thrive quietly amid the noise. This subchapter serves as a guide for cultivating that indispensable form of wealth: the wisdom to speak—and the wisdom to remain silent.

Ending Where You Began: What Matters Most Now?

The act of investing, particularly in the dynamic and often volatile world of cryptocurrency, is more than a pursuit of profit; it is a reflection of personal values, intentions, and ultimately, a story about what matters most to the individual investor. As this chapter draws to a close, it invites the reader to return—intentionally and thoughtfully—to the genesis of their engagement with crypto. This return is not an act of retreat but of grounding, asking a profound question: *How has your original intention evolved, and what remains central to your vision?*

This question challenges investors to move beyond the noise of price swings, market trends, and external pressures. It insists that the foundation of all financial decisions must be clarity about purpose. When one's investment strategy is tethered to a well-examined 'why,' every action gains coherence, and every outcome—whether gain or loss—contributes meaningfully to a larger life narrative. Such clarity is not static; it evolves alongside the individual's changing circumstances, knowledge, and aspirations. Revisiting intentions periodically is, therefore, a crucial discipline, preventing the drift into speculative frenzy or emotional reactivity.

To illustrate, consider a professional who initially entered the crypto space motivated by a desire for financial independence. Over years of engagement, that motivation might deepen into stewardship—not just of wealth, but of the underlying technologies and communities that crypto empowers. Alternatively, a young student might begin investing out of curiosity or peer influence but come to see it as a vehicle for supporting causes aligned with their values, such as decentralisation, privacy, or financial inclusion. These evolving intentions illustrate how investing can be an *autobiographical practice*, an ongoing dialogue between one's inner values and external actions.

This evolution demands critical self-reflection. What were the hopes and fears that shaped your first foray into crypto? Have those emotional undercurrents shifted? Are you still investing for the same reasons, or have your priorities changed? Recognising this allows for the alignment of portfolio construction, risk tolerance, and engagement style with authentic goals. It also provides resilience;

when market turbulence threatens confidence, a grounded 'why' serves as an anchor, reducing impulsive decisions and reinforcing patience.

An essential element of this reflection is acknowledging what *no longer* serves you. Perhaps certain assets no longer resonate with your vision, or the pursuit of quick gains has given way to a commitment to long-term value creation. Shedding investments or behaviours that contradict your evolving priorities is not failure but growth. It is a form of *financial decluttering* that parallels personal development, clarifying what to hold onto and what to release.

Anchoring investing within a broader life context also invites consideration of balance. Crypto need not dominate one's identity or daily focus. Instead, it can occupy a meaningful place alongside relationships, health, intellectual pursuits, and community. This holistic view reduces the risk of over-identification with financial outcomes—a source of stress and distraction—and instead fosters *stewardship as a form of mindful participation.* Your portfolio becomes a tool for sustaining the life you envision, not a measure of your self-worth.

Practical prompts can guide this ongoing self-inquiry: What personal values do your current holdings embody? How does your engagement with crypto advance your broader life goals? In what ways might your strategy be refined to better reflect who you are today? Such questions transform investment from a transactional endeavour into a reflective practice, deepening both understanding and satisfaction.

Moreover, this reframing encourages a shift in how success is measured. Traditional finance often prioritises metrics like return on investment or market share. Here, success encompasses *meaning*, *alignment*, and *peace of mind.* It acknowledges that the greatest value may lie not in wealth accumulation alone, but in cultivating *agency*—the ability to live according to one's principles and to contribute positively to the world through those principles.

The implications of this mindset extend beyond the individual. When more investors adopt intentional, values-driven approaches, the collective market culture evolves. Speculation gives way to stewardship; volatility is tempered by patience; community trust strengthens. This shift is not utopian but pragmatic, rooted in the recognition that markets are human systems shaped by the behaviours and values of participants.

Finally, ending where you began is not an endpoint but a cycle. The clarity of purpose gained through reflection informs future decisions, which in turn invite new reflection. This dynamic process ensures that investing remains a living, evolving practice rather than a mechanical task. It empowers readers to engage with crypto not as passive actors buffeted by external forces but as conscious agents crafting a financial life that supports their most meaningful aspirations.

In embracing this approach, investors find themselves equipped not only for the technical challenges of the crypto landscape but also for the profound personal journey it entails. The narrative of what matters most—anchored in clarity, authenticity, and growth—becomes the true compass guiding decisions amid complexity and change. This is the quiet power of intentional investing: it transforms wealth from an abstract goal into a lived, purposeful reality.

Conclusion
The Ledger You Can't See

As this exploration draws to its close, it becomes clear that the journey has never been merely about arithmetic gains or speculative manoeuvres. What has been charted here is something subtler and, perhaps, more demanding: a meditation on mastery. Not mastery of markets in the narrow sense, but mastery of one's own stance toward wealth, risk, and freedom in an era increasingly shaped by decentralisation and digital flux. The ledger that matters most is not found on block explorers or tucked inside a hardware wallet; it is etched in quieter places—habits, convictions, and the discipline to act with intention. The pivot is profound: what so many seek from without is, in fact, already alive within. The decentralised promise is not only technical but deeply personal, almost philosophical.

To recognise this, one must tilt the gaze away from familiar yardsticks—balance sheets, candlestick charts, portfolio ratios—and look inward. The truest ledger is made not of tokens but of values and the choices that spring from them. It is unseen, yet indelible, and it becomes a compass when the outer world turns cacophonous with hype and panic. In a culture addicted to spectacle and acceleration, the deliberate cultivation of thoughtful wealth becomes, strangely enough, an act of rebellion. To step aside from the current of frenzy is itself a declaration of sovereignty.

Mastery, in this sense, is layered. Of course, it includes competence: how custody works, what tax law demands, why certain protocols deserve caution. But it refuses to stop there. It is also ethical, emotional, narrative. To master wealth is to own the story of one's financial life, to acknowledge uncertainty without surrendering to it, to practise patience when the crowd thrashes in volatility. Such mastery marks the difference between the fleeting opportunist and the enduring steward. It asks you to stop seeing yourself as a passive consumer of market swings, and to recognise instead that you are authoring a financial life—one thread in the larger tapestry of your existence.

Viewed through this lens, even decentralisation itself alters shape. It is no longer only a matter of networks and code. It is the discipline of choice, the ability to act in alignment with one's values rather than being jerked about by external demands. The decentralised self is not defined by the tools at hand but by the clarity with which those tools are wielded. That insight, echoing through the earlier pages, culminates here: sovereignty is not granted by technology, but by the stance of the individual who employs it.

Of course, none of this arrives by accident. To build such an inner ledger requires practice. It demands revisiting your motives, questioning your appetite for risk, recognising when you are chasing noise rather than nurturing conviction. It means measuring growth not just in balances but in composure, discernment, resilience. And this shift bears practical fruit: steadiness in turbulent markets, protection against emotional whiplash, a sense of coherence that anchors decisions in something larger than profit.

History, if one cares to look, offers countless examples. Families, communities, investors who resisted the lure of glittering booms and endured through busts—what kept them intact was not luck but a framework internalised, a discipline carried quietly over years. Their wealth was not always loud, nor was it necessarily admired at the time, but it lasted because it was rooted in mastery. And mastery, even without wealth, carries its own form of liberation.

So, the invitation in these closing pages is simple yet formidable: claim your internal ledger as the record that matters most. Let it be imperfect, let it evolve, but let it be yours. It should grow with experience, accommodate vulnerability, and reflect a life not free from difficulty but shaped with intention. For in the din of markets and the spectacle of modern finance, it is silence, reflection, and deliberate action that emerge as the rarest currencies of power.

To step into this perspective is to move differently through the decentralised age. Not as a bewildered spectator, forever reacting, but as a grounded authority—custodian of wealth that exceeds numbers, participant in a practice that endures. The ledger you cannot see is the one that steadies all the rest. To tend it carefully, day after day, is perhaps the most profound act of sovereignty any of us will ever make.

We close with a meditation

Mastery, not money. Self-trust, not speculation. These are the real currencies in a world obsessed with digital wealth. As the final pages of this guide unfold, they invite a profound reflection on what this journey through the cryptosphere has truly demanded—not just financial acumen, but an internal ledger of discipline, clarity, and autonomy. Beyond the charts, the tokens, and the market noise lies an invitation to reclaim authority over one's own narrative. The decentralized world does not simply decentralize assets; it decentralizes power. The authority that many sought externally resides within. *This is the ultimate ledger—the one you carry inside, invisible yet unassailable.*

To understand why this internal ledger matters, one must first acknowledge the cultural forces that shape our relationship with wealth and power. The modern world is a cacophony of noise—ceaseless updates, trending tokens, social media boasts, and viral hype. Within this clamour, the temptation to measure success by public performance, rapid gains, or external validation is overwhelming. Yet, those who have endured market cycles and technological upheavals consistently reveal a counterintuitive truth: quiet, thoughtful wealth, cultivated with patience and reflection, is the most radical form of resistance against the chaos of our times. *In choosing silence over spectacle, discretion over display, the investor enacts a powerful sovereignty.*

This sovereignty is not merely about protection from external threats or market volatility—it is a spiritual and psychological achievement. The mastery of self-trust emerges as a response to the relentless uncertainty inherent in decentralised systems. Unlike traditional finance, where intermediaries mediate risk and provide institutional assurances, the decentralized realm demands individual responsibility at a granular level. The learner evolves from a passive participant to an active guardian, holding keys not only to digital assets but to personal autonomy. This evolution is a reclaiming of agency, a refusal to outsource trust blindly to external actors or ephemeral market sentiments. *Such self-trust is forged through education, experience, and a disciplined engagement with complexity.*

Realising that the most important ledger is internal reframes how one perceives risk and reward. The temptation to chase short-term gains or to be swayed by market sentiment gives way to a long view, where growth is measured not only in tokens but in wisdom. This perspective shifts the conversation from *what* is held to *why* it is held, anchoring financial decisions in a deeper personal vision rather than reactive speculation. This is where investment becomes autobiographical: an extension of one's values, aspirations, and principles rather than a mere pursuit of profit. *By embedding intention within strategy, the investor enacts a form of wealth that transcends numbers.*

Embedded in this internal mastery is an ethical dimension rarely discussed in mainstream finance. Decentralization, at its core, proposes a reconfiguration of power structures, seeking to distribute authority away from centralised entities toward individuals. This redistribution is not automatic; it requires vigilance, education, and an unwavering commitment to personal responsibility. The quiet investor is also a conscientious steward of a broader vision—one that embraces privacy, autonomy, and sustainable growth over the allure of rapid speculation. *In this light, quiet wealth becomes a statement of integrity and a refusal to capitulate to the performative pressures of contemporary culture.*

Real-world examples illustrate how this internal ledger operates. Consider the early adopters who weathered multiple market downturns, not because they chased trends but because they aligned their holdings with long-term principles. Their wealth accumulation was neither ostentatious nor publicized; it was a private testament to patience and self-mastery. On the other hand, those swept up in speculative frenzies often face not only financial loss but erosion of confidence and trust in themselves. These contrasting outcomes underscore the existential stakes involved—*investing is not merely a technical exercise but a test of character.*

Yet, cultivating this internal authority is neither simple nor instantaneous. It demands continual learning, reflection, and the humility to acknowledge what one does not know. The decentralized world, with its rapid innovation and evolving norms, can overwhelm even the most diligent. Here, *mastery is less about flawless prediction and more about resilience—the ability to maintain clarity and purpose amid flux.* It is a mindset that values steady progress over erratic bursts, calm deliberation over impulsive reaction.

This chapter also challenges the reader to reconsider what it means to be "wealthy" in a digital age. Beyond the accumulation of tokens or the expansion of portfolios lies the cultivation of *quiet confidence*—a state in which financial security coexists with psychological equilibrium. The most radical resistance to a culture that equates worth with visibility and velocity is to embody an economy of discretion, where power is measured by one's capacity to act with intentionality rather than react to external stimuli. *This quiet wealth is both shield and sword, protecting autonomy while enabling meaningful engagement.*

The final pages do not offer prescriptions or definitive endpoints; instead, they invite ongoing inquiry into one's evolving relationship with money, trust, and selfhood. The ledger you cannot see is not static—it is written daily through decisions, habits, and reflections. It is a personal narrative that transcends market cycles and technological trends, offering a foundation upon which true freedom and mastery rest. This understanding reframes the entire journey: the decentralized future is not a promise delivered by technology alone but a possibility realized through individual sovereignty.

As the reader closes this guide, they are reminded that their greatest authority lies not in external validation or market performance but in the quiet, deliberate cultivation of their own internal ledger. *Herein lies the true power of decentralization—a power that no algorithm or blockchain can grant, but only the individual can claim.* This chapter serves as both a meditation and a manifesto, calling for a return to the essential: the mastery of self as the ultimate form of wealth in a world beset by noise and uncertainty.

About the Author

Rowan Hale writes at the intersection of technology, psychology, and personal sovereignty. With a background in digital culture and a lifelong interest in how people build meaning through systems, Rowan approaches the world of crypto not as a hype-driven marketplace but as a mirror of deeper human patterns—trust, risk, and resilience. Their work invites readers to step back from the noise and engage with emerging tools from a place of clarity and intention. A quiet advocate for financial literacy in an age of distraction, Rowan spends most days researching long-term thinking, cultivating digital minimalism, and helping others navigate complexity without losing their center.

www.ingramcontent.com/pod-product-compliance
Lightning Source LLC
Chambersburg PA
CBHW031348230926
51848CB00002B/435
* 9 7 8 9 3 7 1 7 7 2 6 7 9 *